THE DHARMIC LEADER

Leadership Anchored
in Hindu and Buddhist
Secular Core Values

JOHN V. PETERSON, PhD

© Copyright 2012, John V. Peterson, PhD

All Rights Reserved.

No part of this book may be reproduced, stored in a retrieval system, or transmitted by any means, electronic, mechanical, photocopying, recording, or otherwise, without written permission from the author.

ISBN: 978-1-60414-550-2

Published by Fideli Publishing Inc.
119 W. Morgan St.
Martinsville, IN 46151

www.FideliPublishing.com

Table of Contents

SECTION I
THE DHARMIC LEADERSHIP MODEL

CHAPTER 1

Introduction 1
    Premise 2
    Current Situation 3
    Emerging Need 5
    Advocates, Not Followers 6
    What Is the Dharmic Leadership Model? 7
    To Whom Does Dharmic Leadership Apply? 8
    What Is Its Relevance? 9
    Pause to Reflect 10

CHAPTER 2

General Characteristics of the
Dharmic Leadership Model 11
    Based on the Secular Core Values of Hinduism
        and Buddhism 11
    Focuses on the Leader, Not the Advocates 12
    Organized Into Four Sections 13
    Flexible 15
    Pause to Reflect 15

CHAPTER 3

The Leader's View of Reality 17
- The Illusion of the Perceived World 18
- Each Moment Is Unique 19
- Change Is Constant... 20
- Embrace Diversity... 20
- The Presence of Good and Evil 20
- Pause to Reflect 21
- Summary of the Differences in the
  Two Views of Reality.. 22

CHAPTER 4

The Leader's Relationship to Self 25
- Get in the Game 26
- Actions Have Consequences 32
- Work for the Results, not the Rewards............................. 33
- Be Alert 37
- Lead a Moral Life 40
- It's Not About You... 41
- Pause to Reflect 45

CHAPTER 5

The Leader's Relationship to Others 47
- Advocates Need to Grow 47
- Interrelationships Are Important 50
- Emotional Outbursts Have Consequences...................... 53
- Advocates Have Unique Needs 55
- Pause to Reflect 55

CHAPTER 6

The Leader's Relationship to Nature 57
    The Duty to Respect and Preserve the
        Natural Environment 60
    Pause to Reflect 64

CHAPTER 7

Application of the Dharmic Leadership Model 65
    Dharmic Leadership in a Real-world Situation 65
    Management Tools 71
    Pause to Reflect 76

CHAPTER 8

Synopsis of the Dharmic Leadership Model 77
    The Leader's View of Reality 78
    The Leader's Relationship to Self 79
    The Leader's Relationship to Others 80
    The Leader's Relationship to Nature 81
    The Next Step Implementation 81
    Pause to Reflect 84
    Become a Dharmic Leader 85

SECTION II

THE FOUNDATIONS OF THE DHARMIC LEADERSHIP MODEL

CHAPTER 9

Definition of Terms 89

CHAPTER 10

History of Dharmic Philosophy
and Its Relevance Today 93
    Brief History of Dharmic Philosophy 93
    Relevance of Dharmic Philosophy in the West
        in the Twenty-first Century 101
    American Transcendentalism and
        Western Nature Writers... 101
    Quantum Mechanics 109
    Summary of the Relevance of Dharmmic Philosophy
        in the West in the Twenty-first Century..................... 115
    Pause to Reflect 116

CHAPTER 11

Two Views of Reality 117
    The Western, Objective View of Reality............................. 118
    The Dharmic View of Reality 122
    Pause to Reflect 133

Endnotes 135

References 139

List of Figures

Figure 1 — The Four Rings of the Dharmic Leadership Model.........14

Figure 2 — The Leader's View of Reality..18

Figure 3 — The Leader's Relationship to Self...26

Figure 4 — The Leader's Relationship to Others...................................48

Figure 5 — The Leader's Relationship to Nature...................................58

Figure 6 — Structure of a Simple Decision Tree...................................72

Figure 7 — Reduction in Manpower Decision Tree............................73

Figure 8 — Structure of a Simple Cause-and-Effect Diagram............74

Figure 9 — Example of Cause-and-Effect Diagram.............................75

Figure 10 — Shiva Nataraja.. 112

Figure 11 — Shiva Nataraja detail.. 113

List of Tables

Table 1—A Comparison of Newtonian Reality
with Dharmic Reality..23

SECTION I

THE DHARMIC LEADERSHIP MODEL

CHAPTER 1

Introduction

- *Are you a leader who cares about people and who values relationships between yourself and other people?*
- *Do you have a holistic view of the world and a concern for the sustainability of a thriving natural environment?*
- *Are you a leader of an organization that is conducting business in India?*
- *Are you interested in the organizational application of Hindu and Buddhist secular core values?*
- *Have you not found any leadership models that align with your values and view of the world?*

If you said "yes" to any of these questions, the *dharmic leadership model* may be for you. This model presents an alternative to existing leadership models. The dharmic leadership model is a values-based model that draws upon core secular Hindu and Buddhist values that adherents have followed for more than three thousand years. This unique approach to leadership draws upon the concepts of dharma, karma, non-attachment, *māyā*, and the belief that all beings are a manifestation of a unified, ultimate reality that underlies all of existence.

Section I of this book describes the core values and behaviors that reflect the dharmic leadership model. The dharmic leadership model is organized into four sections: the leader's view of reality, the leader's relationship to self, the leader's relationship to others, and the leader's relationship to nature. Section II presents an in-depth description of the philosophy that provides the foundation for the dharmic leadership model. The two sections can be read independently.

PREMISE

Leadership is personal; it is a combination of a leader's inherent traits and learned behaviors borne from personal value sets. While inherent traits are important, they are beyond control or development by a leader. Such traits become a precondition and a foundation for leaders to build upon in the form of values, behaviors, and actions. Ninety percent of each individual's core values are locked in by age ten. During children's teen years, their imprinted values are tested and confirmed. People use these values throughout their lives to judge other people, interrelationships, and events. Only a significant emotional event will alter those values during adulthood. Because all interrelationships and interactions with the world are filtered through the lens of personal values, it is hypocritical to not consider values as an integral part of leadership.

People do not become leaders on their own volition; followers select leaders. People may aspire to leadership, but they reach their goal only when followers accept them as leaders. Research by leadership scholars has found that people become leaders when the expression of their values and behaviors strikes a positive chord as they interact with people. Leaders become leaders as a result of the outward expression of their core values, the strength of their principles, and the level of trust they create through the convergence of their values and the expression of those values in the form of compatible behaviors.

To be effective leaders, individuals should adopt a leadership model that aligns with their personal values and personality. Whether articulated or not, a leader's behavior expresses a personal set of values. As situations occur, every human being decides how to react at that moment. The decisions people make must be justified in their own minds, and the decisions on how to react must align with their value sets. Therefore, it is appropriate for leaders to adopt a leadership style that can be personally justified and be in alignment with their own values.

CURRENT SITUATION

Leaders have existed throughout human history. Leadership scholarship and the creation of leadership models, however, began in the twentieth century as a response to the leadership development needs of large, complex organizations created as a result of the industrial revolution. Leadership scholars have identified nine major leadership models and more than eighty leadership "brands," leadership models that fill a specific niche and are marketed through books, CDs, tapes, and seminars. There is variety among these models.

- Some models focus on the inherent traits of the leader, the premise that leaders are born, not made. Also known as the "great man" theory, trait theory emphasizes intelligence, self-confidence, determination, integrity, and sociability.

- Other models focus on learned skills, specifically technical, human, and conceptual skills.

- Another grouping of leadership models emphasizes the differences in leadership styles. In these models, leaders are categorized by the methods used to elicit the desired performance of the followers. Terms used in these models include authoritarian, paternal, indifferent, and opportunist.

- A fourth grouping of leadership models focuses on leaders as agents of change. In these models, leaders have the traits and skills to set a vision for the future of the organization, the charisma to inspire and motivate followers, and the empowerment of the followers to implement change.

- A fifth major category of leadership models emphasizes the core values of the leader and followers, with the leader taking the role of servant and steward of the organization. These models emphasize ethical leadership, the empowerment of followers, limited use of the power of the institution, empathy, unconditional acceptance of all stakeholders, and an emphasis on trust and respect.

There is commonality among almost all leadership models in one key respect. They reflect Western value sets, especially values based on an objective view of reality. Also known as a Newtonian view, the objective view is based on the perception that the world observed through the senses is the only reality. It is also believed that this reality is not only objective, but it is also rational, ordered, comprehensible, and the same for everyone. There is, however, a totally different view of reality that undergirds the value sets of a large segment of the world's population: the Hindu and Buddhist view of reality. The Hindu/Buddhist view of reality has generated a set of core values that are distinctly different from those presented in leadership models based on Western values. As globalization and international commerce increases, there is an emerging need for a leadership model that reflects this differing view.

- The dharmic leadership model is a values-based model that has its foundation in the Hindu/Buddhist view of reality. Additionally, as can be noted by its name, the concept of dharma is one of the key values. Dharma will be described in greater detail later in the book. Briefly, however, dharma is the process of a person fulfilling a responsibility through the analysis of the situation, the development of a plan, and the implementation of the action in an ethical manner.

EMERGING NEED

India is emerging as a new global economic power in the twenty-first century as both recipient and benefactor of the growing trends of globalization and internationalization. The economic policy reforms mandated by the International Monetary Fund in 1991 CE became the turning point in India's emergence from its self-mandated exclusion of foreign investment. Foreign investment began in India in the early 1990s, but it was accelerated by the need for IT engineers to solve the Year 2000 (Y2k) computer problem. The technical capability demonstrated in Indian engineers who assisted in solving the Y2k software changes showed Western companies that India was a cost-effective source for superior IT technical expertise. As a result, foreign investment in India mushroomed in the late 1990s and early twenty-first century. The explosion in Indian IT development centers and customer-service centers created a new middle class in India that emulated middle-class Westerners by adopting a consumer-oriented economy. This new middle class sparked another even more broad-based economic boom around a variety of consumer goods. Major consumer-goods manufacturers based in Japan, Europe, and the United States began meeting this demand by building factories in India.

As a natural progression, Indians began moving into positions of leadership within these global corporations. As the new paradigm developed, a deficiency in leadership scholarship emerged. Most Indians are either Hindu or Buddhist, and it became important for leaders' leadership style to align with Indian value sets, because values shape how a person reacts to situations. The common, secular core values of Hinduism and Buddhism are very different from the Western core values that support most leadership models. No leadership models reflected the core dharmic values of Hinduism and Buddhism. This deficiency created a need for a new leadership model.

Many Western business leaders must interact with leaders of Indian companies. Western leaders must therefore understand Indian culture and the impact of Indian value sets on business decision making. Hindu and Buddhist core values permeate secular Indian culture. Many films, plays, and songs thematically express the tenets of dharma and the karmic consequences of either good or evil actions. These values are the common underlying thread of all daily inter-relationships, including those that occur in a business setting. The dharmic leadership model establishes a context for this understanding.

ADVOCATES, NOT FOLLOWERS

The dharmic leadership model proposes the use of a new term to define those who support a leader: *advocate*. Leadership scholarship refers to those who support or take direction from a leader as a *follower* and the study of followers as *followership*, a natural use of terminology "to follow the leader." The term *follower*, however, can infer personal characteristics that are at odds with the core values of the dharmic leader. In relationship to the leader, the term *follower* implies a subordinate or subservient role, a role from a position of inequality. While it is true that in an organization, the leader is responsible for the viability of the organization and is, as a result, the ultimate decision maker, this responsibility does not come from a position of personal superiority. It comes from superiority of the position within the organization, not the superiority of the person.

Dharmic philosophy believes that every person is equal and that every person functions from a position of free will. The term *follower* does not imply equality or free will, but the term *advocate* does. An advocate for a position implies support for a position or a set of values based on the conscious decision that the values are of merit and can be supported. An advocate functions from a position of equality and free will; therefore, the dharmic leadership model will refer to those who support or report to a leader as advocates.

WHAT IS THE DHARMIC LEADERSHIP MODEL?

This book introduces a new leadership model that reflects the secular core values of Hinduism, Buddhism, and Vedānta—a philosophy that serves as both the dominant school of Hinduism and a stand-alone philosophy. Known as the dharmic leadership model, it draws upon the common secular core values of dharmic-inspired philosophies to identify values and behaviors that can be applied in a leadership context. This leadership model is an alternative to other leadership styles; it does not claim to be better than the other models or be a replacement for them.

You will notice that this book is not long, which is intentional. The dharmic leadership model is not a complex model with many distinct elements. Even though it is simple in its organization, it is demanding on the leader in its implementation. In the process of adopting this model, you, as a leader, must evaluate the following:

- how you view the world
- what the core values are that shape how you view yourself in the world
- and how these core values are expressed as behaviors between you and your advocates.

Take your time reading this book. Interact with the information in it. As you read the concepts, pay attention to your thoughts. Do you agree or disagree with specific elements? Ask yourself why. What are your values? Are they different from the values presented in this book? Are you comfortable with the values present in the book? If so, why? Take notes; write in the margins. Write down what you believe. The notes do not have to be well thought out. Write down your thoughts at that moment, however sketchy they might be. They will mature over time. You may even find that your initial thoughts at the beginning of the book change by the time you finish the book.

TO WHOM DOES DHARMIC LEADERSHIP APPLY?

The emergence of India in the global economy has raised the world's awareness and recognition of India's rich philosophical heritage. In the West, there has been a renewed interest in Hinduism and Buddhism, and to a lesser extent, Vedānta. There are 300 million Buddhists worldwide and a little more than one million in the United States. There are 900 million Hindus worldwide, with approximately three-quarters of a million in the United States. Many others are not counted in these statistics but are people who adhere to the value sets represented by these two philosophies yet do not call themselves Hindu or Buddhist. As Westerners have more involvement with India in a business environment, there is a potential for an increase in interest in these value sets by non-Hindus and non-Buddhists.

WHAT IS ITS RELEVANCE?

The core dharmic roots of Hinduism, Buddhism, and Vedānta are three thousand years old. A question could be raised regarding the relevance of a three-thousand-year-old Eastern philosophy in the West in the twenty-first century. Already there is a historical precedent relative to the impact of the Vedas and dharmic philosophy in the West. The philosophy expressed in the Hindu and Buddhist writings had an impact on the writings of the American transcendentalists and the nature writers that followed them. This mid-nineteenth-century movement had an impact on the North American psyche that developed into part of the core values of the North American culture. The relevance of an ancient philosophy in the twenty-first century is established through the discoveries of quantum mechanics. Research of quantum mechanics in the twentieth and twenty-first centuries spawned a new philosophical view of the world and all of existence. Through the use of extremely sensitive instrumentation, research physicists are making discoveries that support two-thousand-year-old Buddhist philosophy. These relationships are addressed in greater detail in later chapters.

PAUSE TO REFLECT

Dharmic philosophy encourages people to be mindful and aware of their external surroundings as well as their inner thoughts and feelings. To build mindfulness successfully, people must take time to reflect on what they have experienced and what they think. Each chapter of this book closes with the reminder to stop and take time to reflect on what you have read. Take notes on topics that you want to research further. Write down your questions and your thoughts.

What do you think of what you read in this chapter? Do you think there is a need for a leadership model that reflects the core values of Hinduism and Buddhism? Do you think some of your core values align with these values?

CHAPTER 2

General Characteristics of the Dharmic Leadership Model

BASED ON THE SECULAR CORE VALUES OF HINDUISM AND BUDDHISM

The history of leadership scholarship reveals a progression of leadership theory through defined stages. The stages range from a focus on leader traits or skills as the earliest stages, scientific management and an emphasis on leadership excellence in the middle stages, and, ultimately, an emphasis on values, spirituality, and a holistic view of leadership in the most recent stages. Research in leadership scholarship has shown that values-based leadership models primarily focus on Western values. Existing values-based leadership models do not address core values associated with Hinduism (including Vedānta) or Buddhism—the primary dharmic philosophies emanating from the Indian subcontinent. The purpose of the dharmic leadership model is to address this gap in leadership scholarship.

The core values of Hinduism, Buddhism, and Vedānta can be interpreted as spiritual values. These spiritual values can be addressed in either a religious or a secular context. The non-religious elements of spirituality can be separated from religion and applied in the workplace. In this context, spirituality in the secular world is the lens through which people interpret and apply their moral and ethical values. The dharmic leadership model is based on this secular interpretation of spirituality. Even though it is a values-based model, it does not deny the existence of traits or skills. The dharmic leadership model recognizes that all leaders have unique skills and traits. No specific sets of skills or traits, as defined by some leadership models, however, are required to be a successful leader. Charisma, intelligence, and flexibility may help in some situations but are not necessary for the leader to be successful.

FOCUSES ON THE LEADER, NOT THE ADVOCATES

The dharmic leadership model is purely a leadership model. It is not a "followership" model; neither does it contain elements of how advocates are expected to respond. This focus is intentional. Some existing leadership models promote uniform relationships between leaders and followers in all circumstances. The dharmic leadership model, however, recognizes that each relationship is unique and varies with the circumstances of the moment. Additionally, it recognizes that many, if not most, of the advocates, functioning from a position of equality and free will, have value sets that differ from the value sets of a leader following dharmic philosophy. Some view a difference in value sets between the leader and followers as a problem, which is not the case in the dharmic leadership model. Recognizing that all people are equal, the dharmic leader takes advantage of the unique skills, traits, and values of each of the followers to assess the situation, decide upon a course of action, and, most importantly, implement a solution.

ORGANIZED INTO FOUR SECTIONS

This values-based leadership model is organized into four sections (Figure 1): the leader's view of reality, the leader's relationship to self, the leader's relationship to others, and the leader's relationship to the physical environment. The four categories represent four major themes that are presented throughout dharmic philosophy. They are best presented within the Bhagavad-Gita, as Krishna counsels Arjuna. These sections can be visualized as four concentric circles. The innermost circle, the one that forms the core for all others, is the view of reality. This is the key element that shapes all other values and behaviors. The second ring is the leader's relationship to self. It represents the leader's own personal core values that guide the leader's behaviors. The third ring represents the leader's attitudes and behaviors to other people; they are the outward expression of the leader's internal value sets. Finally, the fourth circle is the leader's relationship to the physical environment. Leadership in the West has historically treated the natural world as a resource to be exploited. Attitudes are beginning to change, however. In today's world, the relationship between the leader and the natural world is taking on greater importance as the world reacts to the effects of global warming and the need to create a global culture focused on sustainability. More than any existing leadership models, the core values of dharmic leadership align with the trend to create a sustainable environment—sometimes called a green environment—that respects the ecological milieu.

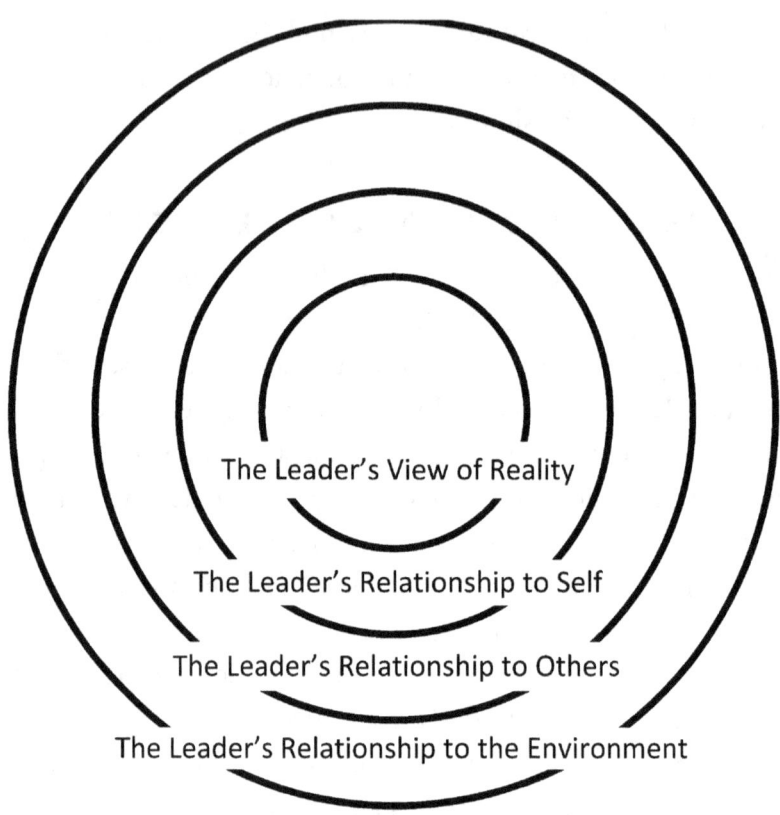

FIGURE 1 —
THE FOUR RINGS OF THE DHARMIC LEADERSHIP MODEL

FLEXIBLE

Even though the values of the leader reflect dharmic philosophy, the implementation of the dharmic leadership model allows flexibility and eclecticism. While some core values represented in this model are unique, others can be commonly found in other leadership models. As a result, the dharmic leadership model allows the inclusion of some leadership tools and team-building techniques that are represented in other, partially compatible leadership models and management tools. The difference between the dharmic leadership model approach and other approaches lies not in the tools but in how leaders and advocates use the tools, how leaders interpret the results, and what actions the leaders and advocates take.

PAUSE TO REFLECT

Even though this chapter is short, take time to reflect on the general purpose and organization of the dharmic leadership model. Think about the organization of the model in four concentric circles. Does this image represent how you already function in life? Do your core values reflect how you see the world? Do your attitudes and behaviors to yourself, to others, and to all of nature reflect your core values? How do you see the world? What are your core values?

CHAPTER 3

The Leader's View of Reality

One unique element of the dharmic leadership model is the perception of reality. Most leadership models reflect a Western, objective view of the world. Leadership values and behaviors are based on the perception that there is one objective reality that is the same for all observers. In this view of reality, the world is fragmented, and every person is an independent entity. In the extreme, this view of reality leads to perceptions of superiority, entitlement, self-importance, and exploitation.

There is a significant differentiation between a dharmic leader and those who follow models based on a Western, objective view of reality. Rather than viewing reality as objective and fragmented, the dharmic leader views reality as an undifferentiated whole in which all people are manifestations of that whole. By viewing all people as interrelated manifestations, it is impossible to perceive others from a position of superiority or to exploit others selfishly without violating the essential core value.

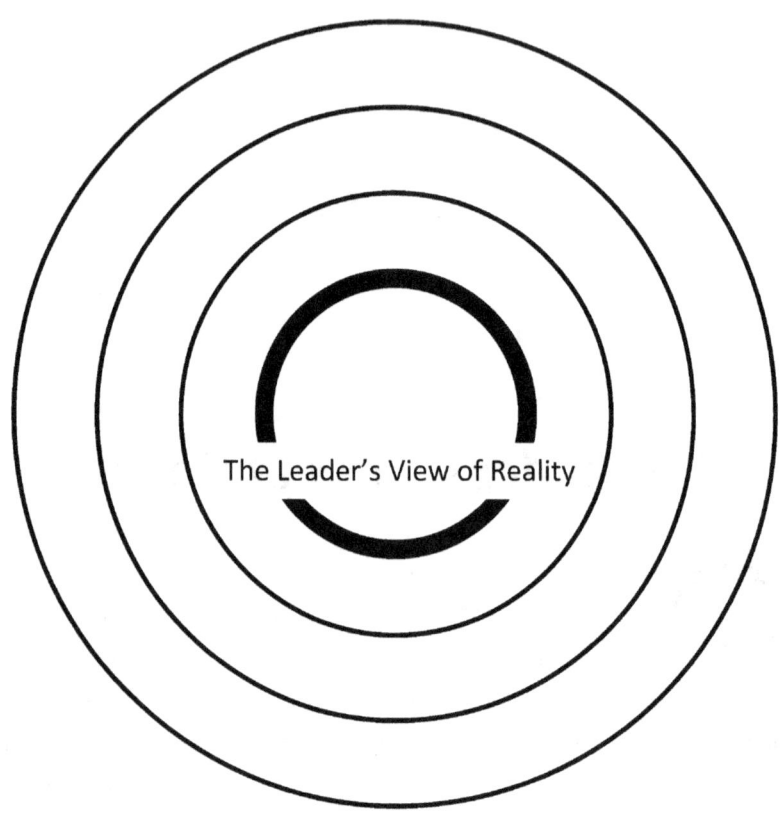

FIGURE 2—
THE LEADER'S VIEW OF REALITY

THE ILLUSION OF THE PERCEIVED WORLD

The dharmic leader views the objective world as māyā, an illusion created by the limitation of the senses. The leader does not deny the objective existence; the leader sees it as the existent perception of reality through the limitations of individual physical senses, experience, and mental capabilities. There is no objective reality; every person has his or her own subjective view of reality that has been filtered through the lenses of perception, capability, and experience. The most pernicious form of māyā is the perception that each person is an independent "I" with an independent ego or consciousness. This illusion creates the feeling in individuals that they are unique beings that react to the world "out there."

The dharmic leader must not fall into the illusion of māyā. The leader must keep in mind that the objective view of the world is illusory and limited. Without the veil of māyā, the leader can perceive the undifferentiated whole and the interrelatedness and equality of all people. The view that there is no singular objective reality is the most important concept in the dharmic leadership model. Each person possesses his or her own reality; each is unique and equally valid. With no one objective view of reality, the dharmic leader must engage the stakeholders to assess multiple perceptions of a situation, to determine the best solution.

EACH MOMENT IS UNIQUE

The Western view of reality sees experience as continuous, uniformly flowing through time. The dharmic leader, however, understands that each moment is unique. Each moment is a unique combination of the circumstances, the people involved, the experiences and feelings of each person, the interrelationships among the people, and the task at hand. Each moment requires that the leader analyze the situation and make the proper decision for that unique moment, the essence of dharma. Because each moment is unique, the dharmic leader must strive always to be "in the moment." The leader must understand the circumstances of the moment through experience and realization, not through detached observation. Understanding comes through immersion in the milieu and the experiential perception of the moment.

CHANGE IS CONSTANT

The dharmic leader realizes that all of existence is impermanent; constant change is the norm. Most people perceive dramatic changes, paradigm shifts. The effective leader, however, fine-tunes the perception to see the subtle changes that occur from moment to moment and over extended periods of time. Rather than viewing change as an independent element to be managed, the dharmic leader views change as an integral element of the interface between each moment. Planning and decision-making must acknowledge the reality of the impermanence of all existence; correct decisions made at one time may not be correct decisions at a later time.

EMBRACE DIVERSITY

The leader who follows the dharmic philosophy needs to be open to unique perspectives and diversity. All people are inherently equal; each person, however, brings a unique set of skills, knowledge, and experience to the team. The equality of individuals as a result of the underlying unity of existence gives credence to the value of diverse perceptions of reality. The leader must be willing to consider differing points of view in the process of making the best decision at that moment in time.

THE PRESENCE OF GOOD AND EVIL

Good and evil are not mutually exclusive. The leader must realize that every person, including the leader, is a combination of good and evil. More importantly, good and evil are not opposite ends of the spectrum; good and evil are relative. Good cannot exist without evil. "The character of man is defined by his actions, his tendencies, both good and bad. Both good and evil have an equal share in defining that character."[1] People often think of good and evil at their polar extremes—the pious person or the malevolent criminal. Consider how lapses in judgment or individual greed have had far-reaching consequences. A momentary lapse in judgment by the crew of the Exxon *Valdez* caused the major oil spill in Alaska in 1989 CE. Similarly, Jeff Skilling and Ken Lay were caring family men who contributed to their community. Their greed, however, motivated them to make decisions based on their self-interest that made them wealthy, but at the same time, set up Enron for failure, to the detriment of thousands of people.

The dharmic leader realizes that good and evil are a continuum and that many decisions occur somewhere in the middle. Every action has both positive (good) and negative (evil) impacts. While the actions may not be as extreme as the circumstances depicted in the Bhagavad-Gita or the "Ramayana," the decisions that today's leaders make are often just as critical to the favorable outcome of the situations they encounter. The effective dharmic leader realizes both the positive and negative impacts of his or her decisions before implementing an action.

PAUSE TO REFLECT

This is the most important place in the book to stop and reflect on what you have read. It is very necessary that you understand the concepts presented in this chapter. The differences in the perception of reality constitute the foundation of the dharmic leadership model and form the primary differences between the dharmic leadership model and all other leadership models available to leaders. Read chapter eleven in section II for a more in-depth description of the two views of reality. Use Table 1 as a reference for review. If a specific concept does not make sense, go back to the description and reread it. If necessary, research other sources until you understand the differences in the concepts.

Take the time to think about how you perceive the world. Have you ever really thought about it, or have you always presumed that the Western view was not only the correct view, but the only view, and therefore there was nothing to think about? What do you think now? Does the dharmic view of reality make sense to you?

SUMMARY OF THE DIFFERENCES IN THE TWO VIEWS OF REALITY

Table 1 summarizes the differences between the Newtonian view of reality and the Dharmic view of reality.

TABLE 1—
A COMPARISON OF NEWTONIAN REALITY WITH DHARMIC REALITY

Newtonian View of Reality	Dharmic View of Reality
The world perceived through the senses is the ultimate reality.	The reality of the world perceived through the senses is not the ultimate reality; it is an illusory, evanescent reality that is limited by the constraints of the senses and is unique to each person. The ultimate reality underlies all existence and is beyond human perception.
Reality is objective, measurable, and uniform from the perspective of all observers.	Reality is subjective. Every sentient being has its own equally valid reality.
Knowledge and understanding of reality is obtained through observation.	Knowledge and understanding of reality is obtained through experience and realization.
The world is fragmented. All sentient beings and non-sentient objects are individual entities.	The world is one unified and interrelated existence.
Experience is continuous. It uniformly flows through time.	Experience is discontinuous. Every moment is unique.
Equilibrium and stasis is the norm for reality at a macro level. Change occurs at the micro or individual level.	Change is the norm for reality. Everything is in flux.
Good and evil are an either/or situation. The goal is for good to overcome evil.	Good and evil are relative. Good cannot exist without the evil.

CHAPTER 4

The Leader's Relationship to Self

People may desire to become leaders; they may even get promoted into positions of authority that give them the venue to demonstrate leadership. Try as they might, however, people do not become leaders on their own. They become leaders when advocates choose to support them. Individuals become leaders when they lead lives that express a behavior that is in harmony with values that appeal to advocates. To be an effective leader following the path of dharmic philosophy, the leader must understand the expected values and behaviors that are the foundation of dharmic philosophy.

Self-awareness of personal values and the expression of those values through proper behavior shape a large part of the texts known as the Smṛti. The Smṛti includes the two epic stories, the "Ramayana" and the "Mahabharata." The "Mahabharata" includes the Bhagavad-Gita, which is often published as a stand-alone document. Both the "Ramayana" and the Bhagavad-Gita emphasize the importance of following individual dharma (duty), responding to karma (cause-and-effect of actions), the

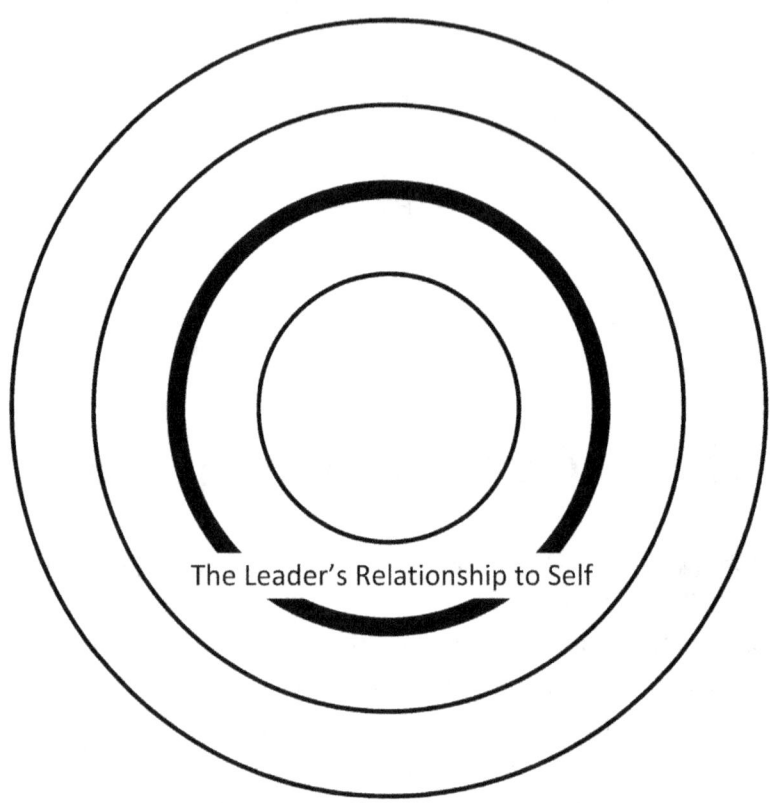

FIGURE 3—

THE LEADER'S RELATIONSHIP TO SELF

impact of suffering as a result of attachments, and the importance of leading a humble life.

GET IN THE GAME

Each dharmic leader must follow dharma. Dharma (duty) is the individual's responsibility to analyze each situation, choose the most appropriate solution reflecting the circumstances of the situation, and take action on the situation. Leaders must be actively involved in life's actions; they must "get in the game."

Within dharmic philosophy, the three defined types, or levels of responses to duty, are known as the three *gunas*. The first *guna* is *sattva*; it is duty done with goodness and virtue. The second is *rajas*, duty done with greed or selfish interests. The third *guna* is *tamas*, duty not done, because of dullness or an inability to act. The ideal form of reaction to duty is *sattva*; duty that is done virtuously with no interest of personal gain. For the Westerner, these three views of duty are conceptually similar to the ethics of Immanuel Kant. Kant emphasized the importance of duty for duty's sake rather than duty for personal gain.

The role of leader inherently defines the person as a decision maker. It is imperative for the leader to analyze each moment and make the most appropriate decision for that moment in time. Additionally, the leader must follow the *guna* of *sattva*. *Sattva* is the performance of dharma with goodness and virtue. Each leader must follow his or her own dharma. Dharma is not to be approached in an anonymous or generic manner; each person's dharma is unique and personal. Another's duty is not to be coveted. As stated in stanza forty-seven of the eighteenth lesson of the Bhagavad-Gita, Krishna reminds Arjuna that it is better for a person to do his or her own duty imperfectly than to do another person's duty well.

On April 20, 2010 CE, the *Deepwater Horizon* drilling rig in the Gulf of Mexico exploded into a fireball. After burning for 36 hours, the rig sank on the morning of April 22nd. Later that day, an oil leak was discovered at the wellhead when an oil slick formed at the surface of the Gulf near the location of oil rig. The leak was not effectively capped until September 19, 2010 after it had become the largest oil leak in history. The *Deepwater Horizon* was owned by Transocean and leased by BP. When man-made disasters occur, the responsible parties need to react responsively and act responsibly to the crisis. The virtuous response considers the impact on all stakeholders including the flora and fauna of the region. Unfortunately, BP's public response to the crisis as expressed by CEO Tony Hayward was self-serving and insensitive to those directly affected by the spill. As the leader of BP, Hayward had the opportunity to express a virtuous corporate culture with his public statements. His most memorable statements, however, characterized a corporation that was more concerned with minimizing its responsibility and its leader who demonstrated insensitivity to the severity of the crisis and the impact on the residents of the Gulf coast. In one instance, Hayward stated that the Gulf of Mexico is a big ocean and that the amount of leaking oil was tiny in comparison to the water volume of the Gulf. On June 1, 2010 CE, Hayward expressed to the media that he would like to have his life back. In early July, he got his wish when he announced that he was resigning as CEO.

What Is Dharma?

Dharma, the performance of one's duties, is one of the primary tenets of dharmic philosophy. Action is an integral part of the dharmic philosophy that believes humans have a responsibility to participate in the progress of life. This participation is the responsibility to assess circumstances, decide on a solution, and take action to achieve the solution. The impact of one's dharma or duty is most tellingly shown in times of crisis. At times of crisis, individuals' doubts and fears cause them to hesitate and question their ability to make the decisions that they know they must make, which is why the Bhagavad-Gita takes place on a battlefield. It is a time of crisis for Arjuna when he is filled with self-doubt. Similarly, the moral fiber of Ramā and the other characters in the "Ramayana" are shown only when the kingdom is thrown into chaos by Kaikeyi's demands.

In daily life, we often see examples of individuals taking the appropriate action without consideration of their own welfare. These people are society's heroes. The New York City firemen who entered the burning World Trade Center on September 11, 2001 CE, and the nuclear power plant workers who risked their lives to prevent a meltdown at the Fukushima Dai-ichi nuclear plant in Japan after the 2011 CE earthquake and tsunami willingly followed their dharma from a virtuous perspective. Business leaders also make virtuous decisions that reflect the greater good rather than the self-interest of the organization. These decisions often go unnoticed, which does not take away from the validity of the actions. The scale or impact of the action is not important. The addition of a five-dollar part to increase the safety of a lawn mower is as ethically important as the decision not to build a potentially profitable factory that will pollute a community. Each action is the correct ethical decision for that moment.

Rāma, the main character in the Ramayana, was trained in the values of dharma; therefore he accepted his duty easily with grace. Arjuna, the main character in the Bhagavad-Gita, appears to not have been trained to understand dharma. It was Krishna's responsibility to educate Arjuna about the three types of duties, to bring Arjuna out of his stupor. Krishna explained the importance of *sattva* to the warrior Arjuna by teaching him that a battle of sacred duty thrust upon a warrior by chance is the best thing that can happen to a warrior. The warrior should rejoice when that situation occurs and not fear the responsibility; that is the warrior's dharma. This perspective is also true for modern business leaders. When the organizations they lead face a time of crisis, it is the responsibility of the leader to take charge and not shirk his or her duty to the organization and its stakeholders. Tony Hayward had the opportunity to demonstrate that he did not fear the responsibility of leadership in the time of crisis. His comments demonstrated his unwillingness to sublimate his personal desires and accept his dharma as BP's leader when the corporation had the responsibility to act virtuously in one of history's largest man-made disasters.

Another component is integral to duty that will be addressed later in this chapter: the concept of non-attachment. Pain and suffering in life are directly related to emotional attachment to people, objects, or even the fruits of action. The second *guna* of duty, *rajas*, emphasizes duty driven by greed and selfishness. Dharmic philosophy states that duty driven by *rajas* leads to emotional attachment. Emotional attachment breeds suffering. When Arjuna asks Krishna what causes a man to be evil, Krishna responds that it is the *guna* of *rajas* that produces greed, desire, and anger—the underlying passions of evil. Vivekananda cogently describes duty in the form of *sattva* when he states the following: "Work for work's sake. There are some who are really the salt of the earth in every country and who work for work's sake, who do not care for name or fame or even to go to heaven. They work just because good will comes of it."[2]

The lure to make business decisions based on greed and self-interest has never been greater. Television and print media have documented the incomprehensible greed of Bernie Maddoff, Marc Dreier, the leaders of Enron, and the manufacturers of melamine-laced baby formula. While these scandals deserve media scrutiny, they are not the only instances of leaders' action driven by greed. Every day, business leaders take the mantra of maximizing profit for the shareholders beyond ethical limits. Their negative actions eventually have negative consequences for customers, employees, other stakeholders, and ultimately, shareholders.

The final *guna* is *tamas*—avoidance of following one's dharma. *Tamas* is also described as dullness and an inability to act. This situation can occur in organizations that have become insular and ossified in their decision-making. Even if the leader of the organization recognizes that its market has changed, the organization is unable or unwilling to react to the changes. Arjuna found himself in this position just prior to a battle with his evil relatives. Krishna chides Arjuna to stop being cowardly; cowardice is shameful and makes a person impotent to action. At other points in his sermon, Krishna reminds Arjuna of the importance of following the dharma of *sattva* and not the dharma of *tamas*. He reminds Arjuna that a man cannot abstain from action and that success cannot be achieved by renunciation.

In the mid-twentieth century, General Motors established a reliance on scientific management tools to manage both production quality and employee performance. Complex forms, flow charts, and committees were developed to document and analyze every aspect of procedures and performance. Over time, the reliance on the management tools created a bureaucracy that became more focused on process and not the end product. As the markets changed, General Motors was unable to adapt. The corporation's matrix management model and committee approval system caused decision making to become ponderously slow. Managers became more focused on protecting their territory and less focused on producing quality products desired by consumers. Senior management attempted to change the culture on several occasions, but the resistance was too great to be overcome. The product that became the poster child of the corporation's emphasis on process over product was the Pontiac Aztek; an ungainly SUV that was panned by automotive journalists and was a sales flop with consumers. Unable to change its culture and react profitably to changes in the marketplace, General Motors was forced to file bankruptcy in 2009 CE. The federal government bailed out the corporation and installed new senior management in the organization with the mandate to invoke a new management style and culture that could nimbly react to future changes. With the shock of the bankruptcy behind them and the influx of new leaders, General Motors was able to seriously address a cultural change that it had previously resisted for decades.

The Importance of Following One's Dharma

Each person's dharma is unique and personal. No one should covet another person's duty. Examples of this position are found throughout important dharmic literature. One of the most succinct occurs in the Bhagavad-Gita when Krishna tells Arjuna that it is better to do one's own duty imperfectly than to do another person's duty well. Each person has a unique set of desires, skills, and experiences. From those assets each person has his or her own well of capabilities to tap when fulfilling dharma. When people attempt to fulfill another person's dharma, they will find frustration, since they may not have the right combination of values and skills to achieve that specific duty.

One of the most frequent examples of individuals who are not following their dharma occurs when parents push children into careers that do not fit the children's interests or skills. For example, self-interest may drive a parent to push a child to attend medical school. The child may have the aptitude and desire to be a history professor, but will acquiesce to the parents' desires. The parents will proudly say to their friends, "Our son is a doctor" without realizing that their son is inwardly miserable for not following his dharma as a history professor.

ACTIONS HAVE CONSEQUENCES

Dharmic philosophy believes in karma—the combination of both action and the consequences of that action. Karma is the process of cause and effect; it is a form of compensation. If a person does a good deed, it will be repaid in this or a future life with a positive result. Conversely, evil deeds are repaid with pain and suffering. "The 'character' of a man is defined by his actions, his tendencies, both good and bad. Both good and evil have an equal share in defining that character."[3] One important aspect of karma is the view that reward and punishment is not divinely meted out, but is defined by each person through his or her actions. It is also believed that people have the opportunity to change their karma for better or worse. Some people in the West equate karma to luck or fate. They lament that they have "bad karma" and have no control over the bad things that happen in their lives, which is not a correct understanding of karma. An individual's karma is a direct consequence of previous actions the person has taken. Each person is responsible for his or her actions and consequences as a result of those actions. Since people are capable of both good and evil, dharmic leaders are vigilant in their actions, decisions, and display of emotions. Karma can affect a leader with both internal and external consequences at the personal, interpersonal, and organizational level.

Competition for desirable jobs is intense. To gain an advantage, people may be tempted to embellish their résumés. They may think that no one will discover that they added an unearned degree or enhanced their performance at a previous job. The unethical action may be justified as a little lie that will not affect anyone. The negative consequences of the action, however, begin almost immediately. The hiding of the truth while promoting the lies creates tension within the individuals' minds as they worry about being caught. This negative consequence – karma – can lead to potential job loss as a result of poor performance and/or discovery that the résumé contains falsehoods.

WORK FOR THE RESULTS, NOT THE REWARDS

Western culture places a strong emphasis on individual recognition, rewards, and awards as accepted forms of rewarding positive performance. Hinduism and Buddhism state that the aspiration of awards and recognition causes emotional attachment to transient objects. The belief that the attachment to egocentricity creates suffering is a primary tenet of dharmic beliefs. The dharmic leader must lead with non-attachment to the fruits of the duty. Non-attachment does not mean the leader must reject personal awards; the leader, however, must not become driven by the desire to earn the rewards. The leader needs to focus only on achieving the goal for the sake of the goal, not the rewards. A dharmic leader must remember that the core values described in this document belong to the leader; the advocates may not have the same core values. As a dharmic leader, you recognize that while you may perform without attachment to rewards, advocates may need to be motivated by the potential of receiving rewards in recognition of their performance.

Some organizations create complex compensation packages for senior executives that tie part of the executive's total compensation to specific organizational outcomes. Compensation rewards include bonuses, stock options, cars, expense-paid vacations, or zero-interest loans. A leader who is rewarded with these forms of compensation must be very vigilant in his decision-making. He must not allow himself to be tempted to make a decision based on potential rewards in lieu of making the most appropriate decision for the situation. Each individual decision may not align with maximizing the performance metrics. Over time, however, correct decisions will result in rewards if the organization is following its dharma and if the performance metrics align with the correct dharma.

Suffering and Attachment versus Non-attachment

Suffering and pain from attachment versus peace and equanimity as a result of non-attachment are important concepts in dharmic philosophy. Humans are motivated by their senses and their emotions. "We *are* the things we possess, we *are* that to which we are attached."[4] Emotions and reaction to the senses cause people to have desires of attachment. Attachment can be emotional attachment to anything, including things (cars, homes, clothes), people (lover, spouse, child), or occupational success (power, money, prestige). For humans, attachment is a lifelong struggle. The goal for individuals should be to realize their attachments and work to break the bonds of those attachments.

Suffering comes as result of change. Attachment causes this form of suffering, the result of clinging to the illusion (māyā) that the world perceived by the senses is true reality. Attachment to illusion breeds attachment to the things, people, and successes that cause daily sufferings throughout life. Nothing is permanent; everything is impermanent. A person desires a new car because it will feed his ego. The person buys the new car and becomes attached to it. The car does not stay new. It breaks and needs repairs; the paint fades; the car wears out. The changes in the car create pain and suffering for the owner. Over time, the owner no longer desires the car; his emotions are drawn to another vehicle, and the cycle begins again.

Suffering and pain also come from attachment to another person. In relationships we obviously have joy, but at times, we suffer pain from disagreement, and we suffer when a loved one dies. Attachment may create short-term positive emotions, but in the long run, it breeds many destructive stress-inducing emotions, including jealousy, anxiety, fear, and disappointment.

Richard Nixon was a successful leader, but he was driven by a dark side—his insecurities combined with his passion for power. In 1972 CE, Nixon was running for re-election as president of the United States. In spite of a commanding lead in the polls, Nixon's dark side drove him to make unethical and illegal decisions. His insecurities and passion for power drove him to approve clandestine operations against his Democratic opponents. One of the operations, the break-in at the Watergate office building, led to his public humiliation and loss of power. His attachment to power resulted in a lifetime of suffering.

Dharmic philosophy believes that the way to avoid suffering and pain is to practice non-attachment. Non-attachment is the opposite of attachment, but it is not the same as detachment. Detachment is avoiding duty. Non-attachment is active involvement in life and doing one's duty without becoming attached to the fruits of the duty. Vivekananda suggested that people should approach non-attachment in the following manner: "Therefore, be "unattached": let things work; let brain centers work; work incessantly, but let not a ripple conquer the mind. Work as if you were a stranger in this land, a sojourner; work incessantly, but do not bind yourselves; bondage is terrible."[5]

Non-attachment is the desired goal. Humans are fallible; the leader must realize that striving to achieve non-attachment is a lifelong struggle. In the Bhagavad-Gita, Krishna not only advises Arjuna to do his duty, but he also advises him to do his duty with non-attachment. Krishna advises Arjuna to be involved in the action but not the fruits of the action. Do what needs to be done, but be equally impartial to failure and success.

Non-attachment has nothing to do with how many possessions you have. It has to do with how emotionally attached you are to those possessions. A person could be a Buddhist monk whose only possession is a begging bowl. If that monk is emotionally attached to that begging bowl, he is no more non-attached than the person living in a mansion who owns several complete sets of exquisite antique china.

Non-attachment is an internal mindset; therefore, it is impossible for an observer to know if a person's actions are motivated by non-attachment or some other intention. There are, however, examples of lifestyles that appear to be based on the dharma of *sattva* and non-attachment to the rewards of the actions taken. A lifestyle driven by non-attachment to the material rewards of business might resemble the lifestyle of Warren Buffet, one of the world's richest men. In his role as CEO and one of the major stockholders of Berkshire Hathaway, Buffett has amassed tens of billions of dollars in wealth. Buffett has expressed a philosophy of investment that emphasizes long-term growth and value in the process of building a company with long-term strengths in the market and the community. He does not believe in an investment strategy that benefits the investor with short-term profits at the expense of the other stakeholders. His investment strategy expresses an attitude of *sattva*; Buffet is investing in a virtuous manner. Buffett's personal lifestyle expresses a non-attachment to the material rewards that are available with his massive wealth. Unlike his peers who have adopted a lifestyle that includes private jets, multiple large mansions in luxurious locations, and exotic supercars, Buffett leads a life that more resembles that of an upper-middle income wage earner. He drives his own American-made automobile, flies commercial, and lives in the same modest home that he bought in 1958 CE. His lifestyle and actions give the appearance that he is driven to do the right things in business and not by the personal desire to accumulate or flaunt wealth. As a result of his actions, phenomenal wealth has come his way and he has earned universal respect.

BE ALERT

In a time of crisis, leaders must have a clear mind to analyze the situation and make the correct decision for that moment (dharma). Leaders cannot allow themselves to be clouded in a fog of anxiety or stress. Mindfulness is the awareness of the external environment and the awareness of what is going on in the person's mind at that moment. The ability to have inner calm and be mindful of the surroundings and one's inner thoughts in a time of stress does not come naturally. The dharmic leader must develop those abilities over time. Patience goes hand in hand with mindfulness and inner calm. It is important for the dharmic leader to display patience. The leader must be the person who remains calm and patient in a time of crisis, to calmly assess the situation and make the appropriate decision.

Mindfulness/Awareness and Inner Calm

Dharmic philosophy believes that each moment is unique, time is not continuous, and understanding comes through experience and realization. Through karma, every action performed by a person has a consequence, good or bad. It is therefore important for leaders to be "in the moment," aware of the world around them, aware of their mental and emotional reactions to stimuli, and aware of the actions they are taking. Mindfulness or awareness has two elements. Mindfulness is awareness of the external environment and awareness of what is going on in the person's mind at that moment. Humans are sensory beings; they interact with the world through their senses. Mindfulness is being acutely aware of sensory reactions, a direct experience. Seeing, hearing, smelling, touching, and tasting are just sensory reactions and nothing more. They are the means of transferring information about the world to the individual without interpretation. Focusing on the immediate sensory sensations forces a person to think about the task at hand and not think about the past or future. In doing so, the person is forced to be aware of his or her mental reactions to the stimuli. This awareness of emotions and thoughts makes the person consciously consider which actions to take.

Focusing on the moment and the mental reactions to the experience creates a sense of inner calm. With inner calm, a person is not controlled by his or her extreme emotions. Extreme emotions, such as anger, frustration, anxiety, or elation, cloud a person's thought processes and place a barrier between that person and other people.

Creating a sense of inner calm is approached at two levels. The first is the calmness that allows a person to think clearly. The second is the aspiration to achieve total inner calm.

In contemporary society, the most obvious examples of individuals focusing on the moment occur in professional sports. The great athletes learn to be "in the zone." If an average person were to stand in the batter's box, a fast ball thrown by a professional baseball player would be a blur. The person may not even see the pitch. Professional baseball players, however, are able to focus on the ninety-five-mile-per-hour pitch. Rather than seeing the ball as a blur, the batter is able to see the rotation of the ball and the undulations of the ball's trajectory. Through focus on the task, the batter can succeed in his task by hitting the ball at the right moment to direct the hit to an area of the field unprotected by fielders.

Leaders in business also have their own situations in which they must focus on the moment. Crises can occur in any business. The leader of the organization in trouble must be the person who maintains a clear mind to focus on the situation, set a plan of action, and lead the implementation of the solution. The crises in business organizations are much more complex than hitting a baseball. Organizations face crises that may place the future of the organization in peril and the livelihoods of employees and their families at risk. In these situations, the need for the leader to be focused and calm is paramount. The crisis could be a singular event, such as a fire in the factory, requiring the leader to make immediate decisions, or the crisis could be a prolonged event, such as the loss of market share or the obsolescence of a primary product. In these cases, the most appropriate action by the leader may be more measured decision-making after analysis of market data.

The second level of inner calm is the aspiration to achieve total inner calm. Dharmic philosophy believes that reality is discontinuous; it exists from moment to moment. Thoughts are also discontinuous. Each thought stirs some reaction in the person. Emotions generate responses that disturb the inner calm of the mind. Total inner calm occurs in those moments between thoughts, when the mind is calm and at peace.

Patience

In dharmic philosophy, especially Buddhism, patience is an important characteristic. Cultivation of patience inherently creates inner calm. Inner calm creates the proper environment for the mind to think clearly, especially in moments of crisis. It is particularly important to foster patience when interacting with other people. Fostering patience allows a person to listen to differing views and benefit from the knowledge and experience of other people. Loss of patience breeds anger. Anger disallows a person to think clearly. When anger arises, a person cannot function with equanimity, humility, or mindfulness. The person's mind closes to the outside world and focuses inward on the negativity fueled by the anger.

Patience is viewed at a second level—the knowledge of and acceptance of karma. With a belief in karma, there is a realization that present suffering is the result of past indiscretions. A person can change the effects of karma only over time; patience is needed to take a long view to patiently change your future over time. To that end, "The Dhammapada"[6] encourages readers to cultivate a patience that endures.

LEAD A MORAL LIFE

Correct moral conduct is an important component in dharmic philosophy. Given that the dharmic leader believes that all people are equally related manifestations of the same underlying reality and that karmic actions generate consequences, it is logical that the leader live an ethical, moral life. When a person understands that everyone is equal and united and that one's actions are rewarded or punished at some point in the future, it becomes apparent that a moral life is inherent in this philosophy. Ethical values and moral actions are displayed in the moment at hand and in the immediacy of reality. Vivekananda described the immediacy of the moment and a person's reactions to each moment when he stated, "If you really want to judge the character of a man, look not at his great performances. Every fool may become a hero at one time or another. Watch a man do his most common actions; those are indeed the things which will tell you the real character of a great man."[7]

The morality of the leader sets the tone for the entire organization. Max De Pree, the former CEO of Herman Miller, established a culture of ethics and morality that transcended all facets of the organization. Throughout two of his books, *Leadership Is an Art*[8] and *Leadership Jazz*[9], De Pree presented a personal morality that included respect for the values, skills, and perspective each employee contributes to the organization. The strength of De Pree's leadership and core values has influenced the mission of Herman Miller beyond De Pree's tenure as CEO. The organization's published core beliefs include the fostering and maintaining of relationships with all stakeholders, encouragement in the decision-making process of the organization, inclusiveness of the talents and potential of all employees, transparency in decision-making, and a focus on environmental sustainability.

De Pree's view of morality in action is similar to the tenets of dharmic leadership. De Pree believed that all individuals were equal, with equal rights to the limited financial and material resources in the world. Therefore, when leaders accept excessive perquisites and bonuses, they are acting in an immoral manner and do not deserve the mantle of leader.[10]

IT'S NOT ABOUT YOU

Leadership is not about you; it is about leading others to complete an action. Some leaders get caught up in the title of their position or the perquisites that come with the power of the position that is on loan to them. They lose sight of their role and focus on the power of the position rather than on the responsibilities of the position. They focus on their ego and make decisions from the position of self-interest. When leaders do such things, they often develop a sense of entitlement that separates them from their advocates.

Many leaders are rewarded with perquisites that feed their ego and lead to a loss of humility. Private elevators, private dining rooms, and travel on corporate jets feeds the executive's ego and leads to a sense of entitlement and loss of humility. More importantly, the leader loses opportunities to interact with advocates at a peer level. Over time the leader may become estranged from advocates and lose their support. Dharmic leaders should eschew the perks that create false class distinctions and separate them from their advocates.

Humility

Pride is associated with attachment; humility is associated with non-attachment. Dharmic philosophy believes that a person's duty needs to be conducted without attachment to rewards or notoriety. Confidence and humility need to be cultivated to give a person the self-confidence to do the assigned duty without needing to strive for recognition. Leaders need to cultivate humility to the point that it is so integrated into their character that they are not conscious of their own humility. When people are conscious of their humility, humility no longer exists. Leaders must control their ego and lead from a position of humility. Leadership is not selected by the leader; it is bestowed on the leader by advocates. The leader needs to recognize this relationship to advocates and lead humbly. Humility should be a natural outgrowth of a dharmic leader's value sets. Humility cannot be intentionally fostered; it must come naturally.

According to Krishnamurti[11], a person who focuses on personal humility is no longer humble. In leaders, humility must develop from the values of non-dualism—the belief that everyone is essentially equal—and non-attachment, especially to the individual ego.

The Dalai Lama serves as a good example of a person who expresses humility. A person asked the Dalai Lama, "Your Holiness, many people feel very possessive about you. How do you handle this?" [12]

The Dalai Lama answered, "You can become obsessive, but that does not make much of a difference to me. I am just sitting here."[13]

The Dalai Lama has always demonstrated humility in all aspects of his life. Even though he is the leader of Tibetan Buddhism, he has never adopted any special trappings or perquisites that would infer any superiority in his position. He has consciously chosen to wear monk's robes and speak of himself as a monk. The Dalai Lama's natural humility and his conscious effort not to materially separate himself from others demonstrates that he understands that the focus of his leadership is not about him but about his mission and his actions. It is clear that his actions are based on virtuous actions and not driven from a position of self-interest. As a result, his words and his actions carry much influence.

EQUANIMITY

Equanimity is the ability to be even-tempered, to be composed. Equanimity is a desired trait or behavior for a person who follows dharmic philosophy. Assuming that a person believes that all of existence is unified, it is necessary to realize that all people are not only equal, but also are related manifestations of the same underlying reality. When a person demonstrates inner calm as a result of the awareness that all people are equal and related, it is impossible not to exhibit equanimity to all people.

Sometimes a leader will show partiality to one advocate over another. When this happens, the leader runs the risk of not seeing interrelationships clearly and possibly not accepting the valid input of the less-favored individual. The clouded thinking could cause the leader to make a wrong decision and follow the wrong dharma.

The dominant theory of leadership for many years was the belief that leaders were born, not made. Under the "Great Man" theory, leaders were assumed to possess certain traits that destined them to be leaders. People who were outgoing, taller, or perceived to be more attractive were automatically perceived to be more intelligent or knowledgeable. Their opinions on topics were weighted more favorably because of their physical traits, rather than any substance that supported the opinion. Even though this theory has been disproven, many people are still swayed by its influence. Leaders are not immune. They can also be influenced by the physical traits of one advocate over another. Leaders must be conscious of this tendency and guard against it. The knowledge, skills, and opinions of all advocates should be considered when formulating a plan of action. The duty of the leader is to engage everyone in the decision-making, to seek out the opinion even of the quiet person sitting in the corner of the room. That person may hold the key to the solution to the problem.

Within dharmic philosophy, there are two levels of equanimity. The first level is the realization that all individuals and groups of people should be treated the same. One group cannot be given preference over another. The second level of equanimity is the desire to benefit everyone, irrespective of their closeness in relationship. Too often in business, leaders make decisions that benefit one or more groups, to the detriment of other groups. Rather than following the *guna* of *sattva* (virtuous decisions), some leaders are driven by *rajas*, the *guna* of greed and self-interest.

The leader who displays equanimity will consider the broader impact on society when making decisions. The expression of equanimity can take many forms. In 1954 CE, J. Irwin Miller, the CEO of the Cummins Engine Company, implemented a plan to elevate the cultural environment for all citizens in the company's hometown of Columbus, Indiana. The corporation founded the Cummins Foundation to improve the quality of public buildings. The foundation paid for the architectural fees of any new school, church, or other public building if the owners of the building agreed to select an architect from a list the foundation provided. Since 1954 CE, the Cummins Foundation has paid more than $22 million in fees for more than fifty buildings designed by world-famous architects. Today, Columbus is known as the "Athens of the Prairie," with buildings designed by Eero Saarinen, I. M. Pei, Richard Meier, Harry Weese, and many other famous architects. The selection of design projects that the Cummins Foundation funded demonstrates equanimity to all citizens of Columbus and the surrounding area. The quantity of architecturally significant buildings has created a cultural milieu that has an equal impact on all citizens.

Decisions that create short-term benefits for the immediate stakeholders to the detriment of other groups are ultimately short-sighted. At some point, short-term decisions that have a broader negative impact will hurt the organization in the long-term. Karma—the law of cause and effect—will prevail. The collapse of Enron and Countrywide Mortgage are two examples of organizations that experienced the impact of karma because of decisions driven by greed.

PAUSE TO REFLECT

Pause to reflect on the contents of this chapter. Do you see the connection between the concepts presented in the dharmic view of reality and the core values presented in this chapter? Are you following your dharma? Do you always follow it with virtue? Do you sometimes take actions that benefit your self-interest at the expense of others? Do you even know when you do it? What do you think of the concept of karma? Do you believe there is a direct correlation between actions and consequences?

Non-attachment is a lifelong struggle for most people. What about you? Do you try to be non-attached? Do you believe that attachment ultimately causes suffering?

What about your ego? Do you believe everyone is equal? Are you humble? Are you patient? Are you alert and mindful to the subtleties of your surroundings and how they change from moment to moment?

Take the time to think about these topics. Write notes to yourself. Identify the areas that most need improvement, and establish a plan of action.

CHAPTER 5

The Leader's Relationship to Others

The previous chapter focused on the values and behaviors by an individual who is aspiring to be a leader following a dharmic philosophy. This chapter focuses on the leader's relationship to others within a dharmic context. There is a reciprocal relationship between leaders and advocates. Given that dharmic philosophy believes that all people are manifestations of the same ultimate reality, leaders must understand the values and behaviors that reflect the philosophy based on nondualism and the karmic relationship of cause and effect.

ADVOCATES NEED TO GROW

The dharmic leader has a duty to others not only to follow his or her own dharma, but also to allow all others the opportunity to follow their dharma. Advocates must also have the opportunity to assess situations, decide upon appropriate action, and implement action. Leaders following the dharmic leadership model cannot be authoritarian in their leadership and decision-making;

FIGURE 4—
THE LEADER'S RELATIONSHIP TO OTHERS

authoritarianism runs counter to dharmic core values. Dharmic leaders must allow advocates to have the chance to learn how to follow their dharma and grow with experience. Using participative management and team-building tools, the dharmic leader nurtures and develops the decision-making skills of advocates and allows advocates to test their skills in increasingly complex circumstances. Individual advocates cannot decide if they have followed the correct dharma (career path) until they have had the opportunity to test the limits of that path. As they experience new situations, some advocates may decide they are following the wrong dharma and choose to change career paths.

The command-and-control form of leadership became dominant in Western organizations, especially manufacturing, early in the twentieth century. In this model, the leader was the only person allowed to consider options, to make decisions, to "think." This style of leadership became prevalent when the majority of workers were expected to perform only manual labor or do repetitive clerical tasks. With the growth of computerization at the workstation, workers no longer perform only repetitive manual tasks. They are expected to analyze situations, make decisions on the spot, and take actions to maintain accuracy, efficiency, and/or compliance. In spite of the changes in job expectations, many leaders try to continue to use the command-and-control model. The application of this model is no longer appropriate in most organizations. Today, a leader who consistently micro-manages or overly controls advocates will not be respected or supported, and advocates will perform actions only under duress. The leader who treats advocates appropriately benefits from a supportive team that willingly supports the leader's actions.

Dharmic philosophy teaches that a person has not only a personal duty, but also a duty to others. This duty is shown in the interrelationship of the individual's personal duty with the duty of other people. Interrelationships among individuals or between individuals and groups are paramount. The duties of two individuals may be different, but they are often interrelated. The failure of one individual to do his duty may cause the other person to be unable to fulfill his or her duty. One example where interrelationships in dharma occur is when the dharmic leader must implement progressive discipline of an advocate for poor performance. If a person is not performing assignments at the expected level, the person may be mired in the *guna* of *tamas,* or performing the wrong dharma. Leaders must perform their own dharma of coaching and disciplining advocates, for advocates to perform their own dharma. The action of disciplining an advocate can be stressful. As a result, leaders often delay performing that necessary task, which becomes a form of *tamas*, reluctance to take action, just as Arjuna was frozen with self-doubt between the two armies. The tools described in situational leadership are useful to dharmic leaders as they help advocates develop skills to achieve their own dharma. The methodology of identifying an individual's specific skills that need development for a specific task is compatible with the core values that see each moment as a unique combination of interrelationships, traits, skills, and action to be taken.

There are times, however, when a person may not have the capability or motivation to achieve certain tasks, even after extensive coaching and training. The person's inability to perform up to required expectations is a form of *tamas*. In this case, leaders must follow their dharma by terminating the advocate from that position or situation. If an advocate tries to complete a task but is unable, the person may be following the wrong dharma without realizing (or wanting to accept) that he or she is following the wrong dharma. It is the responsibility of the leader to recognize this inner conflict and take action to force the advocate's change in responsibilities to give the advocate the opportunity to follow correct dharma and become successful.

INTERRELATIONSHIPS ARE IMPORTANT

The cultivation of interrelationships is integral to the role of the leader. The importance of interrelationships among people within dharmic philosophy is a direct result of the belief that all sentient beings are equal manifestations of a common existence. The Dalai Lama emphasizes that discrete entities cannot be separated outside the context of a complex range of interrelationships. The dharmic leader needs to be conscious of every interrelationship with advocates and other stakeholders. Each interrelationship is unique, based on the skills, values, and experiences of each person.

THE IMPORTANCE OF INTERRELATIONSHIPS

Dharmic philosophy, especially Buddhism, believes that interrelationships among sentient beings are a primary aspect of existence. Dharmic philosophers believe that the complex network of interrelationships is the binding force of the non-dualist view of reality. Discrete individuals functioning independently are a dualist view of reality. Buddhists refer to the interdependent nature of reality as "dependent origination," and it is a core element of the Buddhist view of existence. Krishnamurti states, "The individual exists only in relationship; otherwise he is not; and it is the lack of understanding of this relationship that is breeding conflict and confusion."[14]

The idea of interrelationships ties back to the idea of the unity of all of existence and Indra's jeweled net. When any gem on the net is affected by an outside force, all of the other gems on the net are affected by the interrelationships that tie each gem together on the net. Western philosopher R. Buckminster Fuller characterized how he served as an integral function in the interrelationships surrounding him by stating: "I live on Earth at present, and I don't know what I am. I know that I am not a category. I am not a thing—a noun. I seem to be a verb, an evolutionary process—an integral function of the universe."[15]

The idea of interrelationships needs to be viewed from the pedestrian level of daily interactions to understand the importance of a person's awareness of interrelationships. All people's emotions have a strong impact on the emotions of the people around them. A leader who is open, warm, and caring will create an environment in which the advocates will also be caring. A leader who leads through anger and intimidation, however, will create an environment in which the advocates are fearful, distrusting, and self-centered.

Equality

In dharmic philosophy, each person is a manifestation of the same ultimate reality; each person is equal, just as each gem on Indra's net of gems is equal and each drop of dew equally reflects the rays of the sun. At the phenomenal level, there are differences in people, which are the result of each person's karma—the sum of each person's capability, experiences, good deeds, and evil actions. It is important for the leader to treat all advocates equally, giving equal attention to the lowest of positions as well as the highest, recognizing that each person is doing his or her equally valid allotted duty.

To understand this concept, look at the tasks taking place in a medical surgical suite. Everyone on the medical team—the surgeon, the anesthesiologist, and the nurses—must work together as equal partners, following his or her own duties to complete the surgery successfully. The circle of relationships that have an impact on the success of the surgery extends beyond the surgical team. A second team functions behind the scenes that is just as critical as the surgical team. The facility maintenance team is responsible for maintaining the cleanliness of the surgical suite. Air conditioning systems are a critical element in the maintenance protocol established by the hospital's facility manager. Large volumes of clean, cold, fresh air cycle through the suite to maintain an environment clean enough for surgeries. If one of the workers in the hospital maintenance department did not follow protocol and did not properly service the air conditioning filters in the surgical suite, harmful bacteria could enter the operating room, putting a patient's life at risk. In this case, the maintenance worker's duty to maintain the equipment properly is equal to the surgeon's duty in the action of saving the life of the patient.

Respect for Individuals

The leader who fosters interrelationships and honors the equality of each individual will inherently develop respect for each individual. Dharmic philosophy proposes that each individual is a manifestation of an infinite undifferentiated existence. At the same time, however, the philosophy acknowledges that each person is superficially unique, based on his or her experience and capabilities. Additionally, each individual has his or her own view of reality based on prior experiences and sensory perceptions. At this superficial, phenomenal level, respect for each individual becomes apparent. The leader needs to recognize, respect, and value the differences in individuals, their differing views of reality, their unique capabilities, their situation in life as a result of actions (karma), and their duty (dharma) in life. Quality circles are one management tool that a leader can implement to encourage diverse participation in the decision-making process. Quality circles allow constituents with differing responsibilities at all levels of an organizational hierarchy to meet as peers to address areas of improvement in the organization. Quality circles meet the criteria of dharmic leadership; individuals with diverse backgrounds and unique views of reality meeting as peers to identify areas of improvement, establishing a plan, and implementing the solution.

EMOTIONAL OUTBURSTS HAVE CONSEQUENCES

Dharmic leaders view all advocates and stakeholders as equal, and they respect the superficial, unique skills possessed by each individual. Just as the sun shines uniformly through different colors of stained glass, giving the appearance of diversity and individuality, the equality of each person is shaded by traits, skills, and experiences that have shaped that person in his or her lifetime. The responsibility of the dharmic leader is to maximize all advocates' capabilities to allow them to follow their dharma. At the same time, the leader's responsibility is to honor the underlying equality of each person and treat each person with respect and equanimity.

When interacting with advocates, a leader must exhibit emotional control. Emotional control is not the absence of emotion; it is the fostering of positive emotions and the elimination of negative emotions. To deal effectively with problems, people must think clearly. Focusing on negative emotions clouds the mind and hampers clear thinking. Focusing on positive thoughts, however, creates a sense of contentment. A calm person is able to think clearly.

The need for inner calm was described in the chapter on the leader's relationship to self. When viewed in the context of interrelationships with others, this quality is expressed as a need to have emotional control. The dharmic leader cannot become angry. Anger clouds decision-making and prevents leaders from making decisions with a clear mind.

The most important negative emotion to avoid is anger. Anger prevents the attraction of close relationships, and close relationships are a key element in the dharmic view of reality. "When you get angry, there's no room for logic or reason; you literally become mad."[16] Anger also has the capacity to isolate, to preclude relationships. "Anger has that peculiar quality of isolation; like sorrow, it cuts one off, and for the time being, at least, all relationship comes to an end."[17] According to the *Dhammapada*[18], "Those who hold back rising anger like a rolling chariot are the real charioteers. Others merely hold the reins."

ADVOCATES HAVE UNIQUE NEEDS

At the risk of sounding repetitive, the dharmic leadership model is a leadership model; it does not place any expectations on the advocates, and it does not assume that advocates will follow dharmic values. It focuses on the leader's values and attendant attitudes and behaviors toward other people. Dharmic leaders must remember that most of the advocates will believe in the objective, Newtonian view of reality. They will also expect the rewards and awards that are part of the recognition of a job well done, which is okay. It is permissible for a leader to present rewards without violating the leader's core values. The leader's core values belong to the leader, not to advocates.

PAUSE TO REFLECT

Pause to reflect on how you treat your advocates. Do you allow them the opportunity to follow their dharma? Do you give them the chance to learn and grow? Do you treat them with equality and respect, or do you create an environment in which advocates are afraid to make decisions? What is your reaction to the material presented in this chapter? Do you agree that it is the leader's responsibility to allow advocates to follow their dharma through learning and growing? Do you agree that it is appropriate for the leader to treat advocates with humility and equality? After reading this chapter, will you view the interrelationships with your advocates differently?

CHAPTER 6

The Leader's Relationship to Nature

The non-dualist, dharmic view of reality sees humanity and the entire physical environment (especially the natural world) as part of one interrelated whole. This view is in stark contrast to the Western view that places humanity separate from (and sometimes in conflict with) the physical environment. Since the dawn of the industrial revolution in the West, a conflict has existed between the profit motive of developers and industrialists and the need to sustain and preserve the natural environment. Under the credo that mankind's responsibility is to dominate and subdue nature, virgin forests have been clear cut; mountains have been denuded in strip mining operations; the air and streams have been polluted; animal species have been hunted to near extinction; many other species have become extinct because of loss of habitat; and the global climate is warming. Even now, the efforts to move toward an economy built on sustainability and concern for the natural environment has been driven by legislative mandates rather than a sense of moral duty.

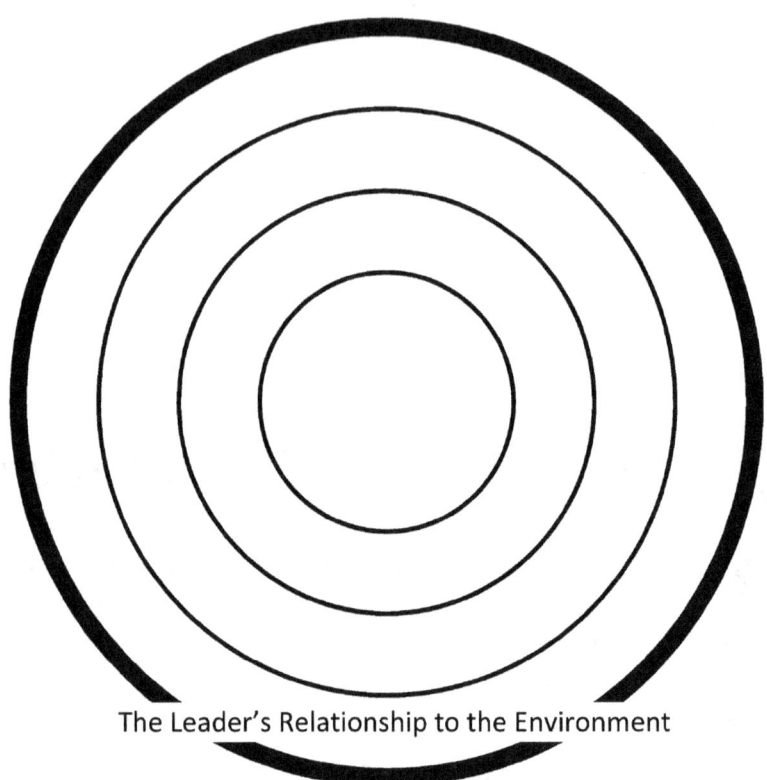

The Leader's Relationship to the Environment

FIGURE 5—

THE LEADER'S RELATIONSHIP TO NATURE

Historically, the drive to legislate pollution controls has been led by naturalists influenced by the American transcendentalists and organizations such as the Sierra Club led by John Muir. The naturalists understood that preservation of the world was a moral issue. They also understood, however, that the only method to implement the necessary changes must come from governmental action. In addition to Muir, Theodore Roosevelt was influential in the significant expansion of the national park system and the implementation of measures to prevent the extinction of American bison. Aldo Leopold wrote about the impact of livestock over grazing on the habitat of wild animals. Rachel Carson raised awareness of the negative impact DDT had on the food chain. Edward Abbey wrote about the impact that power plants had on the air quality of the southwestern deserts and the pollution caused by strip mining in both the West and in the Appalachians. The short-term, human-centric approach to the use of natural resources has created a global karmic cause and effect resulting in a global crisis not only for humanity but also for many other species of animals and plants.

Dharma is the analysis of circumstances, the selection of the most appropriate solution, and the action needed to implement the solution. The impact of dharma at the micro level—between individuals—is described in detail in chapter 5. Dharma is just as important at the macro level as it is at the micro level. Leadership decisions that have an impact on the natural environment can affect many communities beyond the leader's organization; therefore, it is very important for the leader to follow the *guna* of *sattva*—virtuous decisions. Unfortunately, decisions made by many business leaders are based on the *guna* of *rajas*, the *guna* of personal self-interest, rather than the *guna* of *sattva*.

The fragmented, objective view of reality, with the individual separate from and in conflict with nature, is not conducive to a holistic view of humanity's interconnectedness to the rest of existence or its responsibility to other beings. According to Ian McHarg, the cause of this lack of sensitivity to the broader needs of the environment is the result of Western values, which place humanity in an anthropocentric position with a cultural mandate to dominate and subdue (exploit) the natural environment.[19] In spite of the overwhelming evidence and mandated controls, the conflict between virtue and personal/corporate profit continues.

The pursuit of personal self-interest at the expense of the natural environment applies to the micro level as well as the macro level. In the late twentieth and early twenty-first centuries, individuals chose to build large "McMansions" many miles from places of employment. Many of these individuals used fuel-inefficient sport utility vehicles to drive to work individually. The extra use of electricity for the large homes and the consumption of gasoline of the large vehicles in the pursuit of this lifestyle added to each person's "carbon footprint" at the expense of the natural environment.

Changes in approach have occurred, usually as a result of a crisis. Yosemite National Park was created after a dam was proposed to flood the valley. Improvements in farming methods were implemented after the Dust Bowl years in the Great Plains left farmland devoid of arable soil. Pesticides such as DDT were banned when the bald eagle and other predatory birds and animals at the top of the food chain were at risk of extinction from the aggregate effects of DDT throughout the food chain. While the trend toward greater sensitivity to environmental sustainability has continued to increase in the public, resistance to change driven by self-interest by some industries has continued into the twenty-first century. As Western society has responded to global climate change with an emphasis on renewable energy sources, lobbyists for the oil and gas industries have continued to advertise their carbon-based energy sources as the cost-effective, responsible choice.

THE DUTY TO RESPECT AND PRESERVE THE NATURAL ENVIRONMENT

The concept of dharma—an individual's choices and implementation of responses to circumstances—applies to the impact of the natural environment as much as it applies to individual interrelationships. Humanity has a responsibility to preserve the sustainability of the physical environment while also respecting the sentient beings and non-sentient objects that constitute the natural milieu. Humanity is part of nature and relies on the health of the natural world to sustain its existence. With the current concerns about global warming and the pollution of air and water, it is imperative that the dharmic leader exhibit the responsibility of protecting and preserving the natural environment, including a respect for all sentient beings. They have differing, but equal rights to flourish within the natural environment.

There are three defined types of responses to duty: the three *gunas* of *sattva*, *rajas*, and *tamas*. *Sattva*, the preferred approach, is the performance of a duty with goodness and virtue. *Rajas* is the performance of a duty from the position of greed and self-interest. *Tamas* is inaction from an inability to act. Too often leaders have made decisions from the position of *rajas,* in which personal greed has been more important than the greater good of the natural world. At times, some leaders/organizations approach their impact on the environment from the position of *tamas*; they know that they are taking actions that damage the environment, but they do not have the initiative to make necessary changes.

Action that results in a positive impact on the environment is a moral issue. For the dharmic leader, consideration for the impact on the natural world by human actions is more than a moral issue; it is an expression of secular spirituality. Given that a core value for the dharmic leader is a belief that all people, animals, plants, and natural or manmade objects are equal manifestations of a unified ultimate reality, it is the duty of the leader to consider the impact on the environment in the decision-making process.

One of the responsibilities of any leader is the creation of a common vision for the leader's organization. An appropriate time for a dharmic leader to set a common vision for an organization is during goal setting. Recognizing that a large organization can have a greater positive or negative impact on the environment than any individual, organizations must consider the implications of their decisions on the health and sustainability of the natural world. The leader and the organization need to realize that actions, especially those based purely on self-interest, have ripple effects; therefore it is imperative that the leader consider the organization's dharma carefully and follow the path of virtue. The decisions faced by leaders daily are analogous to the choice Arjuna had to make at the beginning of the Bhagavad-Gita. Should he follow the virtuous choice, which entailed greater struggle and risk for the greater reward for his nation, or should he succumb to a personal inability to act and not resist the evil adversary causing the destruction of his nation?

Duty to the Physical Environment

The entire physical environment, including humanity, is part of Indra's net of gems. Since humanity is part of nature and reliant on the health of the natural world to sustain its existence, humans are obligated to protect nature. The protection of nature is not only for the benefit of humanity, it is also for the benefit of all sentient beings. This level of responsibility is known as Universal Responsibility. The Dalai Lama states that he believes that "every act has a universal dimension."[20] When the West was primarily an agrarian society, actions taken in any one community had little or no impact on surrounding communities. With the rampant growth of industrialization, actions taken at a local level can now have global implications. It is the duty of individuals and organizations to consider the implications of their decisions on both a local and global scale.

Universal Responsibility is the process of decision-making that considers the well-being of others. Most leaders learn to make decisions based on the self-interest of the leader's organization. Decision-making based on the concept of Universal

Responsibility runs counter to traditional management training, in which an organization's profit takes precedence over the needs of "others"—those who are not typically considered stakeholders in the organization. The concept of Indra's net of gems has taken on greater importance as man's ability to have a negative impact on the environment has geographically expanded. It is the responsibility of the dharmic leader to consider the needs of all in the process of decision-making for the organization. In the complex, interconnected world of the twenty-first century, the number and breadth of stakeholders has increased dramatically, and the spectrum of variables to be considered in the decision-making process has broadened. A leader who believes in Universal Responsibility is expected to consider the moral and ethical aspects of a decision along with the material and bottom-line elements. The leader is also expected to weigh the impact of a decision on the new range of global stakeholders. By following the concept of Universal Responsibility, the dharmic leader is able to make the correct, virtuous decision that considers the needs of the global community while implementing an action that benefits the organization.

Respect for the Physical Environment

In the twelfth lesson of the Bhagavad-Gita, Krishna teaches Arjuna his responsibility to preserve and protect the environment. It is every person's responsibility to protect all creatures with equanimity. The non-dualist view of reality inherently places humanity as an integral part of all of existence. Humans need to recognize that the world is populated by many species of sentient beings, and the differences among species are a matter of degree, not type. The world, as uniquely perceived by each species, exists for the benefit of all; therefore, humans must respect nature holistically as well as specifically toward each species.

Local and national economies have been built on industries that have not factored in the costs to produce products and services that respect the physical environment holistically. As a result, there have been devastating offshore oil leaks, strip mines that pollute streams and rivers, and clear-cut forests that have damaged or eliminated the habitats of mammals, birds, and fishes. Air and water pollution has changed the world's climate. The lack of progress in making changes as part of the Kyoto Protocol demonstrates the complexity of the problem. No one leader, company, or industry will likely be able to change the current paradigm. It is imperative that many leaders join together, adopt a holistic view of the role of industry, and take action that is virtuous and beneficial to all stakeholders, including those that are non-human, and not retreat to the easier path of self-interest and short-term decisions.

PAUSE TO REFLECT

Pause to reflect on your relationship with the physical environment. Do you see how the dharmic relationship to nature is a logical extension of the dharmic relationship to yourself and others? Do you understand how a dharmic approach to leadership can lead to a more sensitive reaction to the needs of other beings and ecosystems? How have you reacted to nature in the past? Have you been sensitive to its sustainability, or have you exploited it? In your role as a leader, how can you have a positive effect on the care and sustainability of the physical environment?

CHAPTER 7

Application of the Dharmic Leadership Model

DHARMIC LEADERSHIP IN A REAL-WORLD SITUATION

The dharmic leadership model is a values-based model that focuses on relationships. Since it is relationship oriented, it is not limited to interactions within the work environment or between leaders and advocates. The application of the dharmic leadership model need not be limited to crisis or confrontational situations. As Vivekananda[21] stated, the true character of a man is best seen in his most common actions; any fool can rise to be a hero at a time of crisis.

As an example of a values-based, relationship-focused, interchange, a major corporate executive and his wife were traveling from California to south Florida. Because he traveled often, the executive had an upgrade-to-first-class ticket for his wife's use. The first flight was a red-eye from California to Atlanta. As the executive was getting his wife settled in her seat, the person sitting next to her offered to trade seats so that the couple could sit together. The executive told him that he was mistaken; he was not sitting in first class. His seat was back in coach. The traveler said that it did not matter; he would gladly move back to coach. Surprised at the stranger's generosity, the executive graciously accepted the offer.

A few minutes later, another traveler came into first class. Looking into the storage bin above the executive, the traveler angrily demanded to know who owned the briefcase in the bin. When the executive said that it was his, the angry traveler took it out of the bin and threw it in the executive's lap. The executive was tempted to start an argument with the angry traveler; however, after he thought about the consequences—getting thrown off the plane, or worse—and the generosity of the person who gave him the seat, he decided not to confront the angry traveler and find another place to put his briefcase. The flight to Atlanta proceeded without further incident.

While boarding the flight from Atlanta to south Florida, the executive found himself in the same situation as when he boarded the first flight, except in reverse. The executive had a first-class seat. A young couple boarded the plane. The husband helped his pregnant wife get settled into her first-class seat next to the executive. Upon doing so, he told her that he would go back to his coach seat. When the executive heard overheard the conversation, he thought about the generosity of the stranger who had given up his seat so that the executive could sit next his wife, and how that action seemed appropriate. The executive told the husband that he would gladly take his coach seat to let him sit next to his pregnant wife. After initially refusing, the young husband agreed to make the trade and sit next to his wife. After the plane landed, the executive found the young couple waiting for him as he exited the plane. The husband gave the executive his card and told him that he was a senior officer in a large telecommunications company. Because of his generosity, the executive was welcome to call him any time he needed assistance.

The story recounts situations that could potentially occur to anyone who travels regularly. The commonality of circumstances makes this story a good format for describing the application of dharmic philosophy in a specific, real-world context. Granted, we cannot assume that any of the travelers in this story were consciously following dharmic core values; however, the unknown traveler who initiated this process might be the exception. For the executive, the occurrence became a learning experience. The executive learned from his travel experiences and applied the lessons in his office environment with his employees and other stakeholders. The executive learned the importance of paying attention to the needs of others, the benefit of being calm in contentious situations, and the emotional freedom that comes from non-attachment to the perks of privilege. Most importantly, the executive learned that actions have consequences.

Interrelationships

Dharmic philosophy promotes the importance of fostering positive interrelationships with others. The interface between or among individuals becomes the starting point for the exercise of both dharma and karma. If the unknown traveler had not initiated the contact with the executive with the offer to trade seats, none of the three scenarios would have occurred, and none of the individuals would have had the opportunity to follow their dharma. If the executive had not learned from the first encounter, he would not have had the positive interaction with the young couple.

Dharma

Each of the three scenarios demonstrate the application of dharma—the process of analyzing each situation, choosing the most appropriate solution reflecting the values of the situation, and taking action. Action can fall into one of three *gunas*. *Sattva* is duty done with goodness and virtue without interest in personal gain. The second level of duty, known as *rajas*, is duty done with greed or selfish interests. The final *guna* is *tamas*, duty that is not done, because of laziness or an inability to act.

In the first scenario, the unknown traveler demonstrated *sattva*. The traveler assessed the situation and made the virtuous decision. Even after he found out that the replacement seat was in coach, he made the trade without hesitation. For the traveler, it was more important for the couple to sit together than for him to have the comfort of a first-class seat on a red-eye flight.

In the second scenario, the angry traveler demonstrated *rajas*. Rather than choosing the virtuous action of checking his luggage or putting it in an inconvenient spot, the angry traveler chose to take the selfish route of removing the executive's briefcase and putting his luggage in that location for his own convenience. In return, the executive could have responded in like manner and forced the issue by removing the angry traveler's bag and putting his briefcase back in its original place. This action would have undoubtedly led to an argument, with possibly both travelers being removed from the plane. Instead, the executive quickly assessed the situation, including the ramifications, and chose another path. He resisted the urge to fight or argue with the angry traveler and chose to take the path of *sattva* by putting his briefcase in an inconvenient location.

In the third scenario, the executive could have chosen any one of the three *gunas*. He could have been oblivious to the circumstances of the young couple and done nothing. This action would have demonstrated *tamas*. He could have recognized the circumstances and chosen to keep his seat, a demonstration of *rajas*—action taken with a focus on selfishness. Instead, the executive learned from the actions of the unknown traveler on the overnight flight and chose the *guna* of *sattva*. The executive gave the seat to the young husband and sat in coach with no aspirations of personal gain from the action.

The Importance of Allowing People to Follow Their Dharma

The story emphasizes the importance of interrelationships and the importance of allowing people to follow their dharma. If the executive had not allowed the unknown traveler to follow his dharma of taking the coach seat, the executive would not have learned from the experience. If he had not learned from the experience, he might not have chosen the dharma of *sattva* on the next flight, when he volunteered his first-class seat to the young husband.

Karma

Karma is the cause and effect of all actions. In the story, one situation dramatically shows the connection of cause and effect. On the second flight, the executive chose to trade seats with the young husband with no aspiration of personal benefit. The karmic effect of his action, however, gave him the potential of a positive personal benefit in the future. The young husband showed his appreciation for the executive's action by giving him his business card and telling him to call if he ever needed help.

Humility and Non-attachment

Emotional attachment to material possessions and other perquisites that create the image of prestige create suffering. The ability to be non-attached from these possessions reduces a person's stress and anxiety. In this story, the unknown traveler has demonstrated non-attachment by willingly sitting in coach and giving up the comfort and convenience of first class on a late-night flight. There was no expectation of repayment or material reward for relinquishing the better, more desirable seat.

Humility is associated with non-attachment. Confidence and humility need to be cultivated to give people the self-confidence to do their assigned duty without the need to strive for recognition or material reward. The unknown traveler demonstrated humility by willingly sitting in the coach section, even though he had paid for a seat in first class. By his action, he showed through his humility that he was equal to everyone else and not too arrogant to give up the convenience of first-class seating for the benefit of the executive.

Good and Evil

Dharmic philosophy does not say that people are either good or evil; it supports the belief that every person contains the potential for good or evil. The unknown traveler demonstrated the best of human nature by willingly giving up a better seat for a lesser seat on an airplane. The angry traveler demonstrated the evil potential within everyone. The executive demonstrated that both good and evil exist in everyone. When confronted by the angry traveler, the executive had to make a decision—respond in a good way or in an angry, evil way. The quandary of the situation shows that individuals contain the capacity for good or evil. Fortunately, the executive chose to respond positively.

Each Moment Is Unique

Dharmic philosophy states that each moment is unique; time and experience are not continuous. The circumstances and the individuals involved made each of the three scenarios unique. The only linkages among the three situations were the effects of karma that flowed from one moment to another.

MANAGEMENT TOOLS

The adoption of the dharmic leadership model does not require the leader to abandon existing management tools. Several existing management tools can be applied with little or no modification in the paradigm of a non-dualist, dharmic environment. The difference in their usage reflects a difference in core values, rather than a difference in the methodology of the tools. Three examples are briefly described here.

Participative Management

Participative management creates the environment for more people to be actively involved in generating ideas and creating better decisions. The elements of participative management are compatible with the core values of dharmic leadership. Participative management allows each person to have an equal voice in shaping both the individual and collective dharma of the organization. Each person has his or her own equal but unique view of reality and sets of traits, skills, and experience. Total Quality Management, quality circles, and other organized methods to help groups assess a problem, decide on a solution, and implement the action are valuable tools to maximize the diverse input by participants in an organized manner.

Decision Tree and the Fishbone Cause-and-Effect Diagram

Two other effective tools for the dharmic leader are the decision tree and the cause-and-effect diagram that is also known as a fishbone, because the finished diagram resembles the skeleton of a fish. These two tools recognize that each moment and each decision point is unique. They also recognize that decisions have consequences. The tools assist leaders and teams in analyzing complex problems and making the best decision

The decision tree [figure 6] is forward looking. It helps a team anticipate probable results from certain actions. The tree starts with an initial decision point. A branch is drawn for each possible course of action. A new node is placed at the end of each action. The new mode represents a new decision point. Possible actions or outcomes for each initial action are drawn from the endpoint. These branches continue until the team is satisfied it understands the best path to take. Only one path ultimately can be taken.

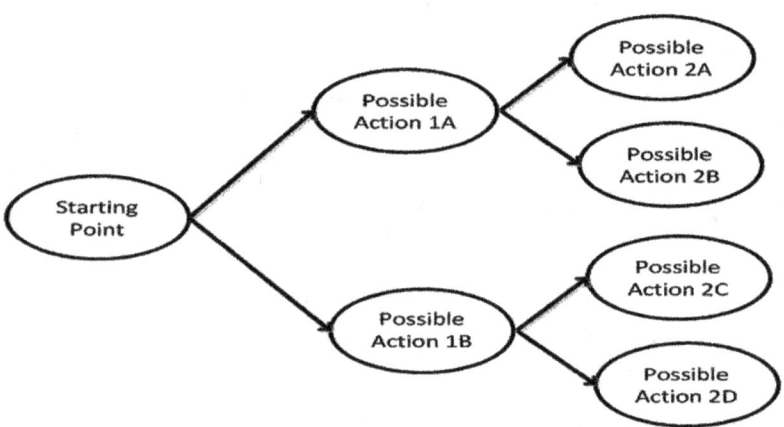

FIGURE 6—

STRUCTURE OF A SIMPLE DECISION TREE

Figure 7 demonstrates a real-world example in which an organization must reduce its manpower. Once that decision is made, the management team must decide if will layoff employees, retain employees but reduce their hours, or select a combination of the two methods [Decision #2]. In this example, the management team decided to select a combination method. The next decision point [Decision #3] is the expanse of the layoff / reduction in hours. Should it be limited to certain departments or be spread throughout the organization? The team decided that the

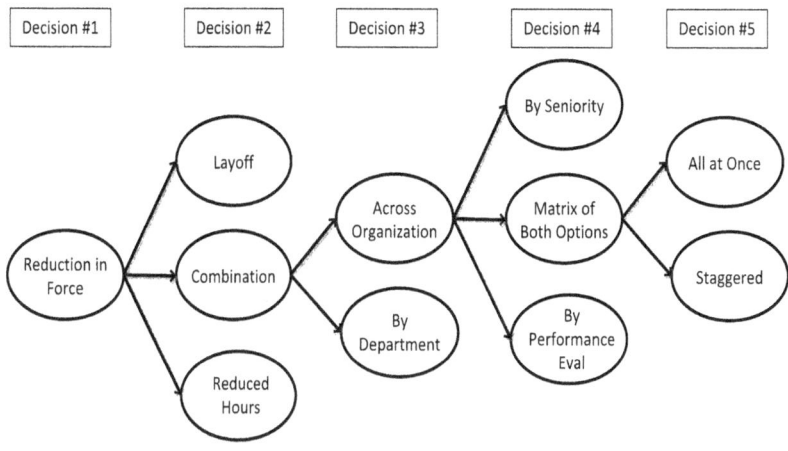

FIGURE 7—

REDUCTION IN MANPOWER DECISION TREE

equitable solution would be layoffs and/or reduction in hours in all of the departments. The fourth decision point is a critical decision that begins to focus on individual circumstances. The management team must decide the criteria for ranking individuals to be affected by the reduction in manpower. Are they ranked by seniority or by performance? If seniority is the sole factor, the organization may be hurt in the long-run through the retention of poor performers and the loss of high performers. An emphasis on performance without consideration of seniority could cause long-term morale issues as a result of the organization appearing to be blind to employee loyalty. The decision made by the management team is to create a matrix that takes both seniority and performance into account in the ranking of the employees. The last decision point in this example is the decision to stagger the reduction in manpower or to have it occur in one action. The decision tree could extend to as many steps are needed to achieve the desired result.

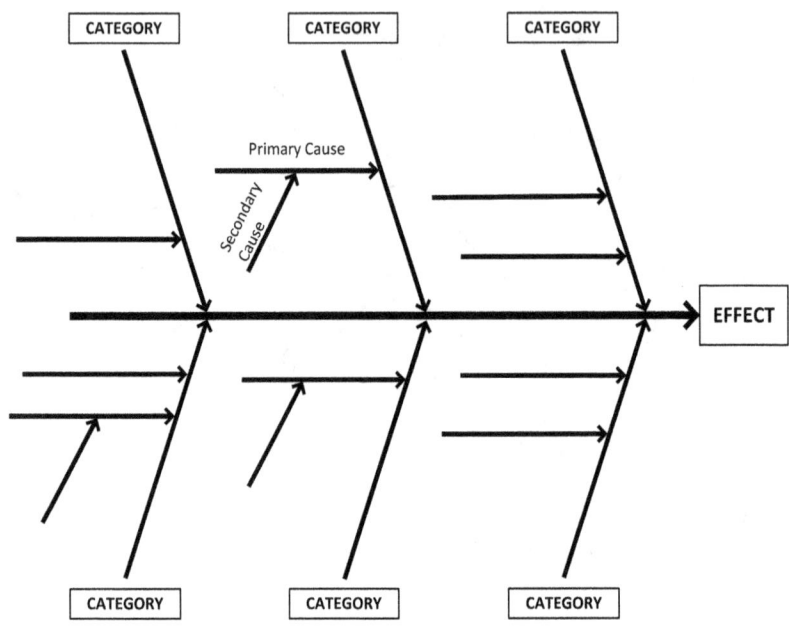

FIGURE 8—

STRUCTURE OF A SIMPLE CAUSE-AND-EFFECT DIAGRAM

The cause-and-effect diagram [figure 8] is backward looking. A certain negative effect that needs to be corrected is known. The task of the team is to identify possible causes for the negative effect. Major categories of causes are identified. These become the primary bones of the fish. Primary causes are shown as horizontal arrows attached to the appropriate category. They are causes for the current effect. They become effects for secondary causes that might contribute to their being a cause of the problem. The secondary causes are the arrows attached at an angle to the primary causes. By working backwards to identify all possible causes, the team is able to identify which causes to address, the ones with the greatest likelihood of solving the current negative effect.

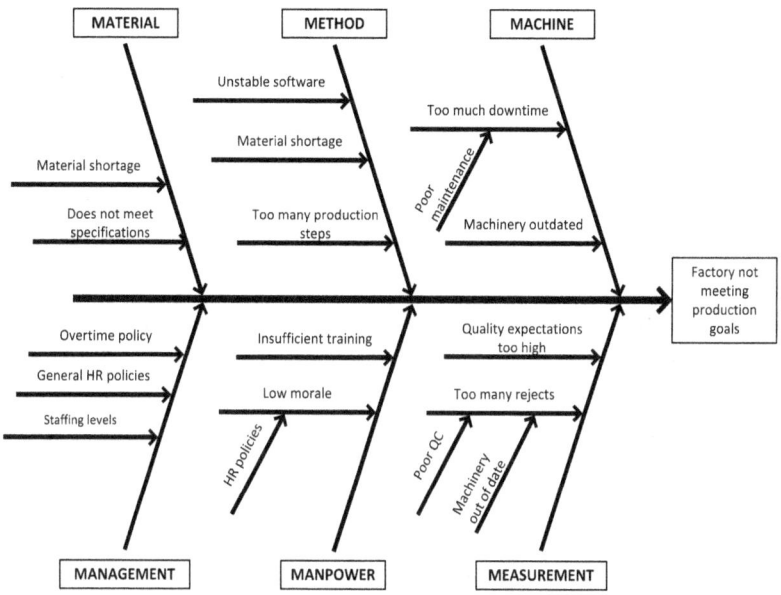

FIGURE 9—
EXAMPLE OF CAUSE-AND-EFFECT DIAGRAM

Figure 9 is an example of the cause-and-effect diagram used to help a company identify the primary causes for not achieving desired production levels. The effect "factory not meeting production goals" is shown in a rectangular box on the right. Potential primary causes are organized along the spine in six groups: Material, Method, Machine, Management, Manpower, and Measurement. In a brain-storming session, representatives from all constituencies identify possible primary and secondary causes for the factory's lack of production. In this example, "Too much downtime" is a primary cause in the machine category. "Poor maintenance" contributing to the downtime of the machinery is shown as a secondary cause. Some causes can be shown more than once if they qualify for multiple categories.

"Material shortage", for example, is shown in both the Material category and Method category. Material shortages could be the result of the environmental factors causing a normally available material to be temporarily unavailable. This cause would be shown in the Material category. Materials that are inherently rare could be listed as a cause in the Method category if an alternative material is more readily available. The evaluation team continues to place possible causes onto the fishbone until the team is satisfied that the most complicit causes have been identified. The use of the cause-and-effect diagram helps the team organize the possible causes and spur discussion regarding the most likely causes for not meeting production goals. The possible causes are prioritized and addressed until the desired effect is achieved.

PAUSE TO REFLECT

In this chapter, you read instances in which dharmic leadership was implemented and existing management tools were presented that can be applied in a values-based leadership model. Does leadership based on dharma make more sense after reading how to apply it in specific situations? Did this chapter cause you to think of instances in which you could have effectively used elements of the dharmic leadership model? Which ones do you already use? How would you need to change your leadership style to incorporate these behaviors or management tools into your daily interaction with people?

CHAPTER 8

Synopsis of the Dharmic Leadership Model

The material in this book does not contain new theories or philosophies; the dharmic core values represent thousands of years of human development. The core values presented are not new to leadership; Krishna in the Bhagavad-Gita and Rāma in the "Ramayana" demonstrated their applicability to leadership situations. In the modern industrialized era, however, Western scholars overlooked these ancient core values while developing leadership models based on Western philosophy that evolved over the past five hundred years. This book reasserts the core secular dharmic values of Hinduism and Buddhism and presents them as an alternative leadership model to modern leaders.

Dharmic leadership is not the only model; neither is it the best model for all leaders. It is, however, an ideal leadership model for leaders whose core values align with the secular dharmic core values of Hinduism and Buddhism. This concluding chapter of section I presents the key core values in synopsis form. By seeing the values in this format, you have the opportunity to see how all the values are interrelated in a cohesive and holistic manner. As you read through these values, pay attention to what you understand and do not understand. Take the time to go back to reread topics in either section I or section II that you did not understand or that did not make sense to you on first reading.

THE LEADER'S VIEW OF REALITY

The Illusion of the Perceived World

Humans are limited by their senses. They can neither hear the full range of sounds nor see the full spectrum of visible light. For many people, the sensory-limited view of the world is the only reality. It is perceived as singular and consistent for all people. The dharmic leadership model is based on the assertion that the sensory-limited world is māyā—an illusion; it exists but is not the true reality.

Each Moment Is Unique

Time is not continuous. Each moment is its own unique milieu, a combination of the people involved, their interrelationships, and the task at hand.

Change Is Constant

Change is not an outside force that is external to the normal operation of an organization. Change is a normal part of the interface between unique moments.

Diversity Is to Be Embraced

All people are essentially equal. Each person, however, has a unique set of values, experiences, skills, and knowledge. The differences are the result of the person's karma. The dharmic leader embraces the diversity within humanity and encourages diverse participation to achieve the most appropriate outcome.

The Presence of Good and Evil

Every action contains a little evil with the good and a little good with the evil. Good and evil are a continuum; decisions lie somewhere in the middle.

THE LEADER'S RELATIONSHIP TO SELF

Get in the Game

Each leader must follow his or her own dharma, the responsibility to analyze each situation, choose the most appropriate solution reflecting the circumstances of the situation, and take action in a virtuous manner.

Actions Have Consequences

Each person is responsible for his or her actions and the consequences of those actions. The philosophy of karma believes that good actions will foster contentment, and evil actions will create suffering and pain. Each person has a choice each time a decision is to be made.

Work for the Results, not the Rewards

Work to achieve the goal, not the rewards that come from achieving the goal. Attachment to rewards breeds suffering and pain. Rewards can be graciously accepted, but they should not be the primary focus of the decision-making or the actions taken.

Be Alert

Be tuned in and aware of each moment. Focus on the moment with patience and inner calm.

Lead a Moral Life

The dharmic leader leads a moral life in which decisions are made from the perspective of a virtuous character.

Control the Ego

The dharmic leader understands that all people are equal; therefore, the leader approaches all people with equanimity and humility.

THE LEADER'S RELATIONSHIP TO OTHERS

Advocates Need to Grow

Advocates need and deserve to have the opportunity to follow their own dharma. Part of the leader's dharma is to provide the opportunity for advocates to grow and find their own individual dharma.

Interrelationships Are Important

Interrelationships are the primary aspect of existence. They are the binding force between sentient beings. One of the primary roles of the dharmic leader is to promote and encourage the strengthening of interrelationships between advocates.

Emotional Outbursts Have Consequences

The dharmic leader retains inner calm, to interact with advocates in a constructive manner. The loss of emotional control, especially through anger and frustration, creates barriers between individuals and weakens interrelationships.

Advocates Have Unique Needs

The dharmic leader remembers that advocates do not have the same values or needs as the leader. Each person has unique needs. Some advocates may not follow dharmic values. The dharmic leader recognizes the needs of the advocates and interacts with them in a manner that satisfies their values and needs.

THE LEADER'S RELATIONSHIP TO NATURE

Dharmic leaders have the responsibility to respect and protect the physical environment. In the capacity as a leader of an organization, the dharmic leader makes virtuous decisions that consider the sustainability of the environment and does not focus only on the self-interest of the organization.

THE NEXT STEP—IMPLEMENTATION

You have now read the description of the dharmic leadership model. The structure and organization of the model is simple; it does not have many individual elements. The task of adopting some or the entire model, however, can be demanding. Implementation of certain elements may take years. A few, such as becoming non-attached, may take a lifetime.

What is the next step? Decide if some or all of the elements in this leadership model are for you. Perhaps you have taken notes as you have read this book. What did you learn about yourself? What do you believe? Do some or all of your values and desired behaviors align with the material in this book? Each person is a product of his or her karma, including you. You have a unique set of values, attitudes, skills, and experiences. To be an effective leader, you must identify your personal set of values and then shape a set of behaviors that mesh with those values, behaviors to use in your interrelationships with other people and the world around you. Remember, the behaviors you exhibit must reflect your inner values, for you to be genuinely perceived and accepted by your advocates.

Your first task is to start at the center circle and identify how you perceive reality. Do you see the world from the objective, sensory level in which everyone and everything is an independent entity? Or do you believe that the phenomenal world is māyā—an illusion that is shaped by the limitations of the senses and the mind? This first step on your decision tree is the most important; it establishes your path in one of three directions.

The first direction is to reject the non-dualist view of reality and realize that your value sets are firmly established in the Western, objective view that the fragmentary, perceived world that is interpreted through the senses is the true reality. In that case, the material presented in this book serves as a potentially interesting alternative view that changes neither your values nor your behaviors. Very few of the ideas presented in the dharmic leadership model will change the way you interact with the people or the world around you. Ralph Waldo Emerson once wrote in his journal that "some books leave us free and some books make us free."[22] If the material in this book did not resonate with you, then it will leave you free, which is okay. You will at least have confirmed what you do not believe.

A second pathway on your decision tree could be the realization that your values align with the non-dualist view of reality—a holistic view of reality. You can accept that all people are essentially equal manifestations of a common, unified reality and that the apparent differences among people are products of their karma perceived through the limitations of your senses. In that case, your interactions with your advocates and the environment will tend to align with the behaviors and actions presented in the second, third, and fourth circles of the dharmic leadership model.

There is one more possible pathway at this stage of your personal decision tree. It is possible that you continue to see the world from the fragmentary, objective view, but still find merit in the dharmic values and behaviors that explain how people relate to each other. In that case, you can build an eclectic leadership model for yourself that reflects your personal values.

The second step in adopting the dharmic leadership model is the assessment of your personal leadership values. Do they align with the values presented in this book? Are you happy with your values, or do you want to change them? Start by making a list of your personal values. Compare them to the values described in the chapter on the leader's relationship to self (the second circle). Note which of your values are already in alignment with the dharmic values. Begin by understanding them and learning how to make them stronger. Next prioritize the remaining values on your list, with the highest priority going to the values that you can most easily adopt and implement. Some values, such as non-attachment, may take years or even a lifetime to change. You can work on these in the background as you integrate other values and behaviors and make them your own.

Once you have identified your prioritized set of values, you must then work on applying the behaviors that reflect the values. For you, as a leader, this step is very important. It is where you develop the very important interface between you and your advocates. Be patient; approach changes in behavior slowly. Advocates need time to react and adapt to your changes in behavior. Remember, they view the relationship from a different perspective; they have expectations based on your prior actions. Even though you are the person initiating the change in behavior, both you and your advocates need time to adapt to your new behaviors. It is also important to be patient in demonstrating new behaviors, to make sure you do not express a new attitude or behavior before you are ready. You must be genuine in your actions. If the expression is not genuine, the action may do more harm than good. Remember that each moment is unique. You must stay alert and "in the moment." You must pay attention to your behaviors and the behaviors of the people around you. Are they the desired reactions? Are you building relationships that are based on respect and equality? Are your actions based on the *guna* of *sattva*—virtuous actions—and not from the *guna* of *rajas*—actions driven from the perspective of self-interest?

Finally, think about how your decisions and actions in both your personal life and professional life impact the natural environment. Do you consider how the decision you make in your personal lifestyle or in your organization negatively impact the world around you? Whether or not you accept the dharma leadership values, you can make the decision to alter your actions and reduce your carbon footprint. "It is up to us as individuals to do what we can, however little that may be. Just because switching off the light when leaving the room seems inconsequential, it does not mean that we should not do it."[23]

PAUSE TO REFLECT

You have reached the end of this section, and this is your last time to reflect on what you have read regarding the presentation of the dharmic leadership model. What do you think? Has the material in this book resonated with you? Has it caused you to think about your values and how they shape your behavior? Have you thought about your values in a new light? What is your next step?

BECOME A DHARMIC LEADER

Become a dharmic leader.

- Look at the world holistically—a world in which every object and every person is interrelated and part of a common existence.

- Be aware of each moment and the circumstances that make each moment unique.

- Nurture interrelationships—treat everyone with equality, respect, equanimity, patience, and humility.

- Follow your dharma—analyze each situation, choose the most appropriate and virtuous solution, and then take action.

- Allow others to follow their dharma—give advocates the opportunity to learn and grow by making choices and implementing solutions.

- Be non-attached—work for the solution, not the reward.

- Recognize that actions have consequences and that everyone has the capacity for good and bad actions. Good actions will reap positive rewards, and bad actions will foster frustration, stress, and suffering.

- Respect and protect the sustainability of the environment — all sentient beings have differing but equal rights to thrive in the natural environment.

If you patiently strive to adopt these values and behaviors, you will become a dharmic leader.

SECTION II

THE FOUNDATIONS OF THE DHARMIC LEADERSHIP MODEL

CHAPTER 9

Definition of Terms

Some of the tenets and terms presented in this book will be unfamiliar to individuals grounded in Western philosophy but will be very familiar to people who follow Hindu or Buddhist philosophy. To begin the process of describing the philosophical ideas presented in this book, this chapter provides a brief definition of dharmic terms. More complete descriptions occur in other chapters.

American transcendentalism. A philosophical movement that formed in the Boston/Concord area in the mid-1800s CE. This movement is not to be confused with transcendental meditation, a movement that was popular in the late 1900s CE. Leaders of the American transcendentalist movement included Ralph Waldo Emerson, Henry David Thoreau, Bronson Alcott, Theodore Parker, Margaret Fuller, and William Ellery Channing. The American transcendentalists were influenced by both Hinduism and Buddhism. They, in turn, had a lasting impact on American nature writers such as John Muir, John Burroughs, Edward

Abbey, and Aldo Leopold. The relationship between dharmic philosophy and American transcendentalism is presented in greater detail in chapter ten.

Ātman. The soul or the self. The core dharmic texts generally equate the Ātman as identical to the Ultimate Reality. Hindu philosophy views the Ātman as permanent and unchanging. Buddhist philosophy is usually silent about the Ātman. When it is mentioned, however, Buddhists state that the Ātman is impermanent and changes in reaction to experience.

Brahman. The Absolute, the Ultimate Reality.

Dharma. Dharma is often translated as duty. In this context, however, duty should not be interpreted in the Western definition of an individual's obligatory service that is expected by a social order. Dharma (duty) is the individual's responsibility to analyze each situation, choose the most appropriate solution reflecting the values of the situation, and take action on the situation.

Dualism. The belief that the world consists of fragmentary elements that have unique identities and existences. Each person, animal, plant, and natural or man-made object is unique and independent. The Western view of reality is dualist. (See non-dualism)

Karma. The cause and effect of all actions. Karma is the belief that good actions are rewarded and evil actions are similarly punished.

Māyā. The illusion that the phenomenal world (the world perceived through the five senses) is the ultimate reality and each individual is an intrinsic, independent existence.

Mokṣa. Liberation from the cycle of birth, life, death, and rebirth. (See samsāra)

Non-dualism. The belief that all people, animals, plants, and natural or man-made objects are part of a unified ultimate reality. The perceived differences in the phenomenal world are the result of limitations of the sensory perceptions. The dharmic view of reality is non-dualist. (See dualism)

Quantum Mechanics. Quantum mechanics is the study of the motion of quanta, especially at the subatomic level. Quanta are packets of energy; quantum mechanics is the study of this phenomenon.

Samsāra. The cycle of birth, death, and rebirth. (See mokṣa)

Smṛti. "That Which is Remembered." This term refers to dharmic literature that is viewed as authored by humans but is not divinely revealed. It includes important epics such as the "Mahabharata", the Bhagavad-Gita and the "Ramayana."

Spirituality. Spirituality can be described as a feeling of relatedness to all beings; it is a sense of transcendence. For some, spirituality and religion are inseparable; spirituality is at the core of religion. To others, spirituality, especially as related to values-based leadership, can be separated from religion; it describes the essence of who we are. Religion is just one element of spirituality. The non-religious elements of spirituality can be separated from religion and applied in the workplace. In this context, spirituality is tied to the secular world as the lens through which people interpret and apply their moral and ethical values. Other elements of spirituality in a secular setting include a sense of interrelatedness and a reverence and respect for nature. The popularity of the nature photography produced by Ansel Adams and

Eliot Porter are examples of the secular nature of spirituality; for many observers, the photographs evoke a sense of transcendence and reinforce the feelings of reverence for nature. The pervasiveness of a secular view of spirituality is evidenced by the popularity of books that combine quotes by authors such as John Muir and Henry David Thoreau, with photographs by Ansel Adams, Eliot Porter, and others.

Śruti. "What was Heard; Revelation." This term refers to the dharmic literature that is divinely revealed. This literature includes the Samhitā, Brāmana, Āranyaka, and the Upaniṣad texts.

Upaniṣads. Upaniṣads literally means "sitting down around," as a reference to the fact that the lessons were orally transmitted by a teacher to pupils who sat around the teacher. The Upaniṣads are the closing chapters of the Vedas and are interpretations of the Vedas.

Vedānta. Vedānta refers to the end of the Vedas, another term used to refer to the Upaniṣads. Vedānta also refers to an orthodox philosophical school of Hinduism that was first developed around 800 CE by Shankara and later revived in the late 1800s CE by Ramakrishna and Vivekananda.

CHAPTER 10

History of Dharmic Philosophy and Its Relevance Today

Throughout the last three millennia, the Indian subcontinent has been the source for many of the world's great spiritual philosophies. This chapter provides a brief historical description of the Vedas and the dharmic-related philosophies of Hinduism, Vedānta, and Buddhism. This chapter also describes how the dharmic philosophies of Hinduism, Vedānta, and Buddhism are relevant in the West in the twenty-first century. The content of this chapter will help the dharmic leader understand the core secular values that form the foundation of the dharmic leadership model.

BRIEF HISTORY OF DHARMIC PHILOSOPHY

The Establishment of the Āryan Society in the Indus Valley

Sometime between 1900 BCE and 1700 BCE, a new culture emerged in the northern parts of the Indian subcontinent. These were the Āryans, part of a nomadic and semi nomadic culture, which lived in small, well-organized communities. Some scholars believe the Āryans moved from the areas that are now Afghanistan and the mountainous countries east of the Caspian Sea through the high mountain passes of the Hindu Kush into the northern parts of the Indian subcontinent. Other scholars believe the Āryans were an indigenous tribe that developed alongside other Indian cultures.

Even though they were nomadic, the Āryans, with their horse-drawn chariots and knowledge of metallurgy, possessed both technology and social structure that were superior to the previously well-developed native Harappā culture, which was already in decline. By about 1700 BCE, the Āryans had supplanted the Harappā society and established its own society throughout the Indus Valley. The Āryan culture created the body of literature known as Vedic philosophy.

Roots of Vedic Philosophy

The term *Vedic* is not an indigenous term in Sanskrit or Indian history. It is a term created by modern Western scholars to describe the philosophy and literature contained in the Vedas. Vedic literature is organized into two major categories: Śruti and Smṛti. Śruti includes the texts of "What was Heard"; they are considered revelation. Smṛti texts are "That Which is Remembered." They are the literature authored by humans but are not divinely revealed.

Śruti

The Śruti literature includes the Samhitā, Brāmana, Āranyaka, and the Upaniṣad texts. The Samhitā are the oldest of all the literature. They are the four Vedas. The literal translation of the word *veda* is "knowledge." The oldest and most important of the Vedas is the Rig Veda.

The Āryans developed more than technology and social order on the Indian subcontinent. They also created a new philosophy that was transmitted through an oral tradition dating back to 3500 BCE. This new philosophy was presented in the Rig Veda. Scholars have generally considered that the first composition of the Rig Veda began around 1500 BCE. The Rig Veda is a compilation of 1,028 hymns that priests used for ritual sacrifices. Between 1500 BCE and 800 BCE, three more Vedas were compiled. The Sama Veda and the Yajur Veda are similar to the Rig Veda in content. The Sama Veda and the Yajur Veda gave instructions to priests on how to sing the verses of the Rig Veda and how to conduct the sacrifices that were integral to Āryan spirituality. The Atharva Veda emphasizes spells and incantations.

The second class of Śrutis are the Brāmanas. The Brāmanas were interpretations of the Vedas (Samhitās) written in prose. These literary compilations were written between 800 BCE and 600 BCE. Sacrifice was an important element of early Vedic rituals. The Brāmanas focused primarily on sacrifice and the symbolism inherent in sacrifice. As a result, the Brāmanas were oriented to the priests and were not popular texts with the average person.

The final two Śrutis, the Āranyaka and the Upaniṣads, were compiled between 600 BCE and 300 BCE. "Āranyaka" translates to "of the forest." The Āranyakas were compiled by priests and sages who sought the refuge of forests to meditate and contemplate the meaning of the Vedas. As with the Brāmanas, the Āranyakas had little long-term impact on the development of dharmic philosophy.

With content oriented to priests and sages on how to properly conduct rituals, the four Vedas do not provide much guidance for the individual in the role of a leader. The Upaniṣads, the last and the most important of the Śrutis, are the first of the philosophical texts to describe core values that a leader can apply. Since the Upaniṣads are the last of the Śrutis, they are also known as the Vedānta—the end of the Vedas. The Vedas are complex and hard for the layperson to interpret. The purpose of the Upaniṣads was to interpret the Vedas in a manner the average person could understand. Upaniṣad literally means "sitting down around." In other words, the listener sat near a sage and listened to the interpretation of the Vedas. Over time, the Upaniṣads became more important than any of the other Śrutis in the development of dharmic philosophy. The Upaniṣads introduced important philosophical elements that became part of the core values of Hinduism that are still prevalent today. Many of these core values are applicable in today's leadership settings. Because the Upaniṣads were approachable and easily understood, they had a significant impact on the Smṛtis, Hinduism, and the specific school of Hindu philosophy known as Vedānta.

Smṛti

The Smṛti literature is composed of stories that are "remembered." The most important and revered of these stories are the epics that demonstrate the dharmic values in contextual settings. They are the "Mahabharata"; the Bhagavad-Gita, which is included in the body of the "Mahabharata"; and the "Ramayana." The Bhagavad-Gita and the "Ramayana" have become the two most influential epic stories in Indian literature, surpassing the importance of any of the Śrutis. Because of the nature of their topics, both the "Ramayana" and the Bhagavad-Gita are primary sources of reference material on the expected core values and behaviors of a leader. Both epic stories depict leaders in crisis situations, to show their value sets and behaviors in times of ethical or emotional crisis.

The "Ramayana" was first composed around 200 BCE. It is the story of the adventures of Rāmā, a prince who demonstrates the Vedic values of dharma, non-attachment, humility, and respect for others as he faces extreme crises in his life. Rāmā, the primary character in the story, is the seventh incarnation of the god Vishnu. Rāmā appears on earth with the primary purpose in life to destroy evil demons and bring the world back into balance. In the course of the story, Rāmā is placed in situations in which he experiences extreme joy and extreme crisis. In each situation, he demonstrates for the observers and listeners of the story the ideal values and actions in times of both joy and crisis. Each vignette is an object lesson that is frequently repeated as homilies on how humans should conduct their lives.

The "Mahabharata," including the Bhagavad-Gita, were composed between 200 BCE and 200 CE. The Bhagavad-Gita is the story of Arjuna, a warrior leader who is suffering from self-doubt on the brink of a great battle against his evil relatives. Krishna, the eighth incarnation of Vishnu, appears as Arjuna's chariot driver. As Arjuna's chariot sits in the open field between the two rows of warring armies, symbolically on the line between good and evil, Krishna delivers a sermon on Arjuna's need to follow his dharma and his karma in the spirit of non-attachment. The story is set in a battlefield to demonstrate to humans that even in the worst of circumstances, they must follow their duty. The battlefield setting also emphasizes that leaders need to learn in times of adversity. In a time of crisis, a person's true character is most tested and the leadership qualities and core values of the leader are most apparent.

Hinduism

Hinduism is the world's oldest spiritual philosophy that establishes a set of idealized values and behaviors for adherents to follow. The Śruti and Smṛti define the core values and expected behaviors of Hindus. As such, the core philosophical base of Hinduism was established by 200 CE, and the Śrutis and Smṛtis—the Vedas, Upaniṣads, "Ramayana," and Bhagavad-

Gita—form the primary sources of philosophical literature for Hinduism. Since that date, philosophical growth of Hinduism has focused on three areas: the expression of devotion through rituals; the expansion of the number gods into a full pantheon of deities depicting specific needs, values, or actions; and the growth of schools of thought that reflect differing interpretations of the core values. Today Hinduism is as much a cultural phenomenon as it is philosophical. The Hindu philosophy is woven into the secular fabric of Indian culture, through the plots in films and literature, in the lyrics of recorded music, and as subject matter in the visual and graphic arts.

Some non-Hindus have misinterpreted the pantheon of deities as an indication that Hinduism is plural-theistic. On the contrary, Hinduism is monotheistic, with Brahman as the ultimate deity. The large number of deities reflects a method of teaching values to an illiterate society. Priests understood that many people could not independently focus on singular values without concrete examples. As a result, a pantheon of deities arose with stories surrounding each deity that conveyed expected values or behaviors. Ganesha, for example, is the remover of obstacles; Saraswati is the goddess of knowledge; Brahma is the creator; Vishnu is the preserver; and Shiva is the destroyer. It is in this context that the mythologies surrounding the characters in the "Ramayana" and the Bhagavad-Gita have been developed. Each character epitomizes a range of desirable and undesirable values and behaviors.

Vedānta

Vedānta is unique among the Indic spiritual philosophies. For some, it is the dominant school within modern Hinduism. For others, it is an independent philosophy. As noted earlier, Vedānta refers to the Upaniṣads—the end of the Vedas. It also refers to a primary school within Hinduism. In the late 700s CE,

Indian philosopher Shankara became disenchanted with the direction of Hinduism. Shankara believed that Hinduism had become too focused on rituals and had lost contact with its core values. He reached back to the Upaniṣads for inspiration and developed a monastic system that emphasized the unity of the individual with the absolute (Brahman) and the suffering as a result of not realizing the world of sensory perception is an illusion (māyā).

The philosophy of Vedānta was re-invigorated in the late 1800s CE by Ramakrishna. His disciple, Vivekananda, introduced Vedānta in the West. In 1894 CE, Vivekananda founded the first United States-based Vedānta Society in New York. Vivekananda also founded the second Vedānta Society, the Vedānta Society of Northern California, in San Francisco on April 14, 1900 CE. Today there are seventeen Vedānta Societies in North America. In the century since their establishment, the Vedānta Societies have grown and changed in response to the needs of the followers. Today the Vedānta Society presents itself as a philosophy with dharmic roots but not a part of Hinduism. According to the website of the Vedānta Society of Southern California, Vedānta is not only the philosophical foundation of Hinduism, but it has also grown in its universal application and appeal. A person can be a follower of Vedānta without being a Hindu. For many Westerners, the first exposure to dharmic philosophy is through the Vedānta Societies in the United States, Canada, and Europe. It is possible for these people to understand and follow the core dharmic values as presented in Vedānta without ever entering a Hindu temple, participating in Hindu religious ceremonies, following Hindu holy days, or understanding the myriad Hindu gods.

Today Vedānta serves as a spiritual base for two distinct groups of people. As described, many people, especially those in the West, see Vedānta as an independent philosophy. At the same time, many devout Hindus worldwide consider Vedānta one of the most dominant schools of modern Hinduism.

Buddhism

Siddhartha Gautama, the eldest son of a powerful Indian king, lived between 563 BCE and 483 BCE. At his birth, a sage declared that Siddhartha would be either a great king or a great spiritual teacher. Fearing that his son would not succeed him, the king protected the prince from the suffering of the outside world and lavished all of life's pleasures on him. Despite his attempts to shield his son, Siddhartha soon learned of suffering as the result of disease, old age, and death. These revelations were a turning point in Siddhartha's life. In the dark of night, he left the luxury of his palace and the intimacy of his wife and child to become a mendicant searching for the meaning of life. For six years, Siddhartha traveled the countryside begging for his food and subjecting his body to many austerities. When he became so weak that he could no longer meditate, Siddhartha realized that he must be healthy and strong to meditate properly. After he gained his strength, Siddhartha decided to sit under a tree until he had achieved nirvana and self-realization. After many days of meditation, Siddhartha achieved nirvana and became the *Buddha*—the One who is Awake. Rather than staying in the bliss of nirvana, the Buddha decided to return to the world to teach others how to achieve an awakened state. From this experience, the Buddha developed the Four Noble Truths and the Eightfold Path. He spent the rest of his life teaching this deceptively simple, but rigorous, philosophy.

Reflecting its Hindu origins, Buddhism shares many of the core values with Hinduism, as expressed in the Śrutis and Smṛtis. The primary difference between the two philosophies lies in how they are practiced. Hinduism is outward looking. It relies on rituals and praying to deities that symbolize specific values and actions. Buddhism, however, looks inward. Rather than relying on rituals or focusing on certain deities, Buddhism emphasizes experience and direct realization. Because of its simplicity and lack of emphasis on ritual or cultural milieu, Buddhism has gained greater acceptance throughout the world.

RELEVANCE OF DHARMIC PHILOSOPHY IN THE WEST IN THE 21ST CENTURY

Dharmic philosophy is a three-thousand-year-old philosophy that originated on the Indian subcontinent. Some people may question the relevance of this philosophy as a source of leadership values in the West in the twenty-first century. This section demonstrates that dharmic philosophy is relevant. The relevance in the West is tied philosophically to the American transcendentalist movement in the United States. The continued relevance is shown with the philosophical tie between the American transcendentalists and the nature writers who followed in their philosophical path.

In the late twentieth century and early twenty-first century, a philosophical view of reality emerged based on discoveries in quantum mechanics. This new philosophy includes elements that are similar to two-thousand-year-old Buddhist philosophy. The new philosophy, based on quantum mechanics, demonstrates the relevance of dharmic philosophy in the twenty-first century.

AMERICAN TRANSCENDENTALISM AND WESTERN NATURE WRITERS

Brief History of American Transcendentalism

The American transcendentalist movement formed around Boston and Concord, Massachusetts, as an outgrowth of the Unitarian Church, centered in Boston. Even though the movement was centered in Boston, its influence extended to New York, Philadelphia, Washington, and Cincinnati. There is no defined start date or end date for the movement; however, its inception is generally considered to be in the mid-1820s CE. The primary movement essentially ended in the mid-1850s CE. A second generation of the movement continued until the mid-1880s CE.

Ralph Waldo Emerson, Henry David Thoreau, and Margaret Fuller are considered the three leading figures in the transcendentalist movement. Emerson, co-publisher of *The Dial*, is considered to be the unofficial leader; Thoreau, the rebellious individualist; and Margaret Fuller, the other influential co-publisher of *The Dial*. Some of the other significant members of the movement include Bronson Alcott, George Ripley, Orestes Brownson, Henry Hedge, and Theodore Parker. One other American writer, Walt Whitman, was not formally considered a member of the American transcendentalist movement, but has demonstrated an affinity with both the transcendentalists and with the core values of dharmic philosophy.

Relationship between Dharmic Philosophy and American Transcendentalism

Dharmic philosophy made an impression on the American transcendentalists in two ways—scholarly and experiential. Ralph Waldo Emerson best exemplified the scholarly approach. Emerson took an intellectual approach to dharmic philosophy, an approach in which the interest in orientalism was an extension of the Unitarian break from Calvinism. The information gleaned from this scholarly approach had an impact on Emerson's philosophy for some period of time, but it did not transcend how he approached daily life. In keeping with his approach to oriental philosophies as a scholarly exercise, Emerson copied long passages of the texts into his daily journals and referred to them in his published works as points of reference.

Henry David Thoreau and Walt Whitman were different. They approached the dharmic philosophies experientially. Rather than copying passages in his journal, Thoreau absorbed and internalized what he read. He then expressed these values in his daily life and in his writings. Similarly, Whitman lived his life as an expression of dharmic values. He firmly believed that the world was perfect and, since he was a part of the world, he was also perfect. In spite of his philosophy, Emerson's life was very traditional; Thoreau and Whitman lived lives outside the norm. Within Concord, Thoreau was considered strange. He was a loner who reveled in his independent lifestyle. In *Walden*, he challenged the lifestyle of others when he wrote how people lived mean lives and that they were asleep to their experiences. Whitman was also independent. His close friend, John Burroughs, wrote that he was "utterly indifferent to what people may say or think."[24] A thorough reading of the works of Thoreau and Whitman yields abundant evidence that both these men were imbued with philosophies that were related to dharmic philosophy. Both men believed in the unity of sentient beings and non-sentient objects; the equality of all people; the realization that the fragmentary, objective view of the world was illusion; ultimate suffering was a result of attachment; and the importance of non-attachment.

Impact of American Transcendentalism on Western Nature Writers

From the mid-1800s CE until today, America has seen a progression of writers who wrote mostly about their observations of nature and the philosophical underpinnings of the man-nature relationship. These writers include, but are not limited to, John Muir, John Burroughs, Theodore Roosevelt, Mary Austin, Aldo Leopold, and Edward Abbey. Many of these writers were apparently inspired by the transcendentalists, especially Henry David Thoreau. The nature writers expressed the unity of existence, the illusion of the fragmentary nature of the phenomenal world, the importance of direct experience and realization, and the acceptance that change is a constant and desired element of existence. Thoreau appears to be a model for many nature writers. Thoreau wrote about what he saw as a scientific observer, made philosophical speculations about the underlying meaning of the world, and spoke out about humanity's abuse and neglect of the natural world. These three themes pervade the writings of most American nature writers.

The progression of philosophical thought from American transcendentalists to nature writers to the general public goes beyond scholarly connections; it was often based on interpersonal connections. One line of interrelationships was very public and well publicized. There was a connection between Ralph Waldo Emerson and a young Walt Whitman. Published letters between the two show how Emerson encouraged Whitman's efforts. John Burroughs and Walt Whitman became friends later in Whitman's life. Their friendship was close enough to allow Burroughs to write a personal biography of Whitman with Whitman's participation. Their close friendship included philosophical discussions that strengthened the writings of both authors. In the early twentieth century, John Burroughs became friends with Thomas Edison, Henry Ford, and Harvey Firestone. The four of them took annual camping trips, calling themselves the Four Vagabonds. Through his friendship with these three industrialists, Burroughs was able to influence the philosophical views of these powerful men.

INFLUENCE ON WESTERN VALUES

Non-dualism and ultimate reality

Reflecting its Unitarian roots, the transcendentalist appropriation of the non-dualist view of reality is understandable. In the 1820s CE, the Unitarians rejected the more orthodox Calvinist orthodoxy, including Original Sin and the emphasis on man as a sinner. The transcendentalists were influenced by the dharmic view that man is inherently divine and that there is no separation between man, the physical environment, and underlying reality. Walt Whitman refers to the unity of all sentient beings and non-sentient objects in many sections of his poetry. It is important to note that the title of his book of poetry, *Leaves of Grass*, reflects a non-dualist philosophy. In stanza 6 of the poem "Song of Myself," Whitman uses leaves of grass as a symbol of the commonality of humanity; no one leaf is better or different from another. He is also showing how leaves of grass show no bias; they grow among everyone without prejudice. Whitman's poetry makes many other references to non-dualism. Additional examples can be found in the first three lines of stanza 1 as well as in stanzas 7, 17, 20, 30, 31, 46, and 48 of "Song of Myself." In those stanzas, Whitman reinforces the unity and interrelatedness of mankind, the importance of equanimity and inner calm, and the need for each person to follow his or her own dharma.

The philosophy of non-dualism (unity of all existence) had a profound effect on Western nature writers. The underlying theme of unity with nature became a focus in the writings of influential nature writers such as John Muir, John Burroughs, Aldo Leopold, and Edward Abbey. John Muir wrote one of the most succinct statements on the belief of the unity of existence: "When we try to pick out anything by itself, we find it hitched to everything else in the universe."[25] In the late twentieth century, influential landscape architect Ian McHarg wrote, "Our eyes do not divide us from the world, but unite us with it. Let this be known to be true. Let us then abandon the simplicity of separation and give unity its due."[26]

Māyā—the Illusion of the Phenomenal World

Ralph Waldo Emerson showed an orientation toward the philosophy of māyā early in his writings. In 1844 CE, Emerson wrote that life is an illusion that we pass through in a series of moments like beads on a string. Each bead has its own hue and shows only what is in focus.

Henry David Thoreau received a set of books on Hinduism in 1855 CE. As a result of access to those books, Emerson's writings began to reflect the influence from these works. The effect of this influence from dharmic sources was shown in the essay "Illusions," which was published in 1860 CE.

Understanding through Experience and Realization

The transcendentalists put greater emphasis on experience and realization in lieu of the detached observation of Newtonian reality. Of the leading transcendentalists, Thoreau appeared to be the most attuned to the importance of personal experience and realization. The most obvious expression of this orientation was Thoreau's two-year residence at Walden Pond. Thoreau explained that he went to Walden Pond to experience life and his reaction to it. He wanted to live deliberately, to experience the essential facts of life and live life to its fullest. Thoreau believed that most people did not truly experience life. He asserted that most people were asleep half the time, and it was important for people to awaken themselves to their existence. In *Walden*, Thoreau explained how he learned to "know beans" through experience. He did not study a book to know them; he gained his knowledge through the experience of planting, hoeing, harvesting, picking, selling, and eating them.

Walt Whitman was another writer who emphasized the importance of personal experience. Whitman expresses this in stanza 46 of "Song of Myself," when he writes that each person must tramp the perpetual journey by himself. No one else can answer the questions; each person must find out the answers independently.

The Randomness and Uncertainty of Constant Change

The transcendentalists and the nature writers were aware that the world is one of constant change. Thoreau stated that all change is a miracle that is taking place every instant.

John Muir perceived the constant change at both the micro as well as the macro levels. On June 6, 1869 CE, he wrote this perception about change at the micro level, "Every rain-cloud, however fleeting, leaves its mark, not only on trees and flowers whose pulses are quickened, and on the replenished streams and lakes, but also on the rocks are its marks engraved whether we can see them or not."[27] Referring to change at the macro level, Muir was amazed at nature's infinite lavishness and the apparent waste through decay. Upon closer examination, however, nature showed that change created new uses for every particle.

John Burroughs also recognized that change occurs at the macro level and often at a rate that is imperceptible to humans.

> Geologic time is the most potent of the gods of change. He wields an invisible hammer beside which the hammer of Thor is a child's toy. Its slow, silent blows break in through granite rocks as big as a house. It is as if the sunbeams or starbeams did it, as if the snows of winter and the dews of summer had the force of dynamite.[28]

Dharma—Duty

Henry David Thoreau was the transcendentalist who took the strongest position on each person's duty. He demonstrated his sense of duty by going to jail to protest paying a tax and then wrote the essay "Civil Disobedience." In "Civil Disobedience," Thoreau[29] wrote, "If I devote myself to other pursuits and contemplations, I must first see, at least, that I do not pursue them sitting upon another man's shoulders. I must get off him first, that he may pursue his contemplations too." Thoreau was also following his duty when he moved to Walden Pond to live by himself for two years. In an action resembling Rama's banishment to the jungle in the "Ramayana," Thoreau willingly went to the forest to meet life head-on to find its meaning. Rama did not choose to go to the forest, but posed with the situation, he willingly accepted the circumstances, understanding that banishment to the forest was his dharma. Rama turned the negative into a positive by emphasizing the opportunity to simplify his life and focus on spiritual growth. Thoreau also chose to use the move to Walden Pond as a means to simplify his life and focus on his relationship to the world.

As could be expected, Henry David Thoreau and Walt Whitman were the two most vocal transcendentalist writers promoting the importance of following one's dharma. They both lived their own lives on their own terms, not worrying about the negative perceptions or castigations from others. Thoreau emphasized that people should not worry about keeping pace with their peers; they may be stepping to the beat of a different drummer. Thoreau also advised readers to be humbly faithful to themselves and not try to emulate another person's skills, responsibilities, or aspirations. This advice resonates with one of the most important verses in the Bhagavad-Gita. In the thirty-fifth verse of the third teaching, Krishna advises Arjuna that it is better to do your own duty imperfectly than to do another person's duty well.

Walt Whitman was perceived as arrogant in the pursuit of his dharma. Whitman's good friend and biographer, John Burroughs, wrote that Whitman's appearance of arrogance came from the belief that nature was essentially good; since he was a part of nature, he was also good.[30] Whitman opens his poem "Song of Myself" with the following: "I celebrate myself, and sing myself, and what I assume you shall assume, for every atom belongs to me as good belongs to you."[31] Later in the same poem, he states, "I exist as I am, that is enough, if no other in the world be aware I sit content, and if each and all be aware I sit content."[32]

Duty to Protect and Respect Nature

As can be imagined, a major focus for some of the transcendentalists and all of the nature writers was humanity's duty to protect and respect the natural world. This attention to the natural world is directly related to the non-dualist view of existence in which there is a holistic, unified view of existence. The duty to protect nature is viewed as a moral issue. Humans are a part of nature. As we are a part of the broad ecosystem, humanity's needs do not take precedence over other forms of life or the natural balance of the world. The Western, objective view of the world places humans separate from the rest of the natural world with a manifest destiny to dominate and subdue nature to the singular benefit of humanity. Reflecting the non-dualist, dharmic view of the world, nature writers such as Aldo Leopold, Rachel Carson, and Edward Abbey wrote essays and books exposing the permanent damage created in ecosystems as a result of humanity's progress at the expense and disregard of the rest of the natural world.

People can show respect for the natural world in several ways. One way is to show that the natural world is neither anthropomorphic nor totally human centered. There are many processes that function independent of humanity's needs. John Muir noted this point when he speculated about the purpose of poison ivy, concluding that it was made for itself. Similarly, Edward Abbey, when speculating on the purpose of a saguaro cactus, concluded that it was there to provide shade for a titmouse.

QUANTUM MECHANICS

Overview of Quantum Mechanics

For several centuries, Newtonian physics, also known as classical physics, was considered immutable. Even today, for many people, classical physics appears to be the valid representation of the world, since it reflects the phenomenal world of the senses. Max Planck, with his theory of quanta in 1900 CE, and Albert Einstein in 1905 CE, with his theory of relativity, created a new physics known as quantum physics. As the twentieth century progressed, physicists made more discoveries that led to quantum mechanics. Quantum mechanics is built upon, but different from, other forms of physics. Classical physics is grounded in theory. Newtonian physics and relativity are both classical physics. Quantum mechanics, however, is different; it is based on probability.

Many elements of quantum mechanics reflect a view of reality and assumptions about existence that mirror dharmic philosophy, both Hindu and Buddhist, from more than two thousand years ago. Besides Krishna's being a central figure in the Bhagavad-Gita, many other stories are told of Krishna's relationship to humanity. One of the stories focuses on his relationship to the gopis—women who are cow herders. All of the gopis of Vraja are in love with Krishna. At night, they dance in a circle with Krishna at the center. The scene symbolizes man's unconditional love for the creator and the personal one-on-one relationship with the creator. Since humans are manifestations of the binding force of creation, the gopis are, in effect, dancing with themselves. The symbolism is similar to the findings in quantum mechanics. Quantum mechanics is discovering that humans are not uninvolved observers; they are actively involved in the creative processes of the world.

Another symbolic connection between dharmic philosophy and quantum mechanics is found in the Hindu statue known as the *Shiva Nataraja* [figure 10]. There is a philosophical link between dharmic philosophy and the research into quantum physics. The *Shiva Nataraja* is a depiction of the god Shiva performing the Cosmic Dance. The Cosmic Dance is the endless cycle of creation, destruction, and rebirth. The large circle surrounding Shiva is symbolic of that endless cycle. Shiva is dancing on a demon, a depiction of Shiva eradicating ignorance and māyā, the illusion of the phenomenal world [figure 11]. The cosmic dance is a dance of joy in all stages of creation, destruction, and rebirth, because the veil of ignorance and illusion has been lifted. A large *Shiva Nataraja* statue is on display at CERN, the European Organization for Nuclear Research. The *Shiva Nataraja* is an appropriate symbol for the work physicists perform at CERN, because they use particle-beam colliders to explore the world at the quantum level. Through the creation and annihilation of hadrons (beams of subatomic particles), physicists are discovering the basic building blocks of the universe. Just as Shiva is breaking the bonds of māyā through the endless cycle of creation, destruction, and rebirth, the physicists, by creating and annihilating particles in colliders, are breaking humans' illusions of phenomenal reality through the discovery of the basic building blocks that are the common foundation for all the more complex elements in the universe.

Relationship between Quantum Mechanics and Buddhism

Non-dualism and Ultimate Reality

The classical physics of Isaac Newton viewed the world as the interaction of individual objects. Individuals who did not have an impact on the outcome of the interactions could independently observe and measure these interactions. The theory of relativity as well as quantum mechanics, however, look at the subatomic level as a series of events and processes. They look at the world in a holistic manner; everything, including the observers, are part of the undivided whole. This view of existence aligns with the dharmic view. In the Hindu and Buddhist view, all sentient beings are manifestations of an undivided whole—Brahman.

FIGURE 10—
SHIVA NATARAJA

FIGURE 11—
SHIVA NATARAJA DETAIL

Māyā—the Illusion of the Phenomenal World

Māyā is the illusion that the phenomenal world consists of individual objects that exist independently in a fragmentary world. Each object appears to be solid and relatively unchanging over time. Except for superficial scratches and dents, a table, for example, appears to be solid and relatively unchanging over time. Quantum mechanics, however, disputes this perception. The table is made up of subatomic particles, the basic building blocks of existence. Research in quantum mechanics has found that the perception of a solid, unchanging object is an illusion. Subatomic particles are not specific objects; they are not similar to motes of dust. Subatomic particles are viewed as "tendencies to exist." Rather than being viewed as identifiable objects, these particles are viewed as probabilities. Since subatomic particles are constantly changing between mass and energy, their state at any point is a probability, which is why the perception of a solid, unchanging foundation for existence is an illusion.

Unique Experiences

The Newtonian view of reality assumes that experiences are continuous and they flow uniformly and cohesively through time. Objects appear to move from point A to point B with a certain velocity and trajectory. Discoveries at the quantum level dispute the Newtonian findings.

Unlike Newton's classical physics, it is impossible to measure both the position and velocity of a particle. The observer must make a choice of which one to measure. Since position or velocity can be measured at one time only, it is impossible to state that the particle at point A is the same one at point B; no motion or velocity was measured between the two points. Since a researcher cannot say with any certainty that the particle that was measured at point A is the same particle that was measured at point B, the researcher must rely on probability, rather than relying on observations

In Newtonian physics, it is believed that an observer can objectively measure occurrences without having an impact on the result. According to quantum mechanics, it is impossible to measure anything without altering the outcome through observation. In essence, researchers are measuring an observer-created reality. The observer is required to decide what to measure. Unlike the philosophy of classical physics, in which the researcher is a detached observer of an independently functioning world, the quantum world requires the observer to choose what to measure before it can be measured. The observer is forced to be part of the process and cannot be independent or detached.

Unique Perspectives and Diversity

Classical physics views time and space as constant and uniform. Everyone observes time and space in the same way, irrespective of time or place; it is viewed as flowing consistently, like sand in an hourglass. Einstein's theory of relativity changed that perception. As the title of the theory suggests, time and space are not constant; they are relative. They are relative based on the location of the observer and the velocity at which the observer is traveling in comparison to the object observed. In classical physics, events occur over time. They develop and change within the context of a one-directional movement of time. In the space-time continuum of the theory of relativity, space and time are static.

SUMMARY OF THE RELEVANCE OF DHARMIC PHILOSOPHY IN THE WEST IN THE TWENTY-FIRST CENTURY

The discoveries of quantum mechanics show the relevance of dharmic philosophy in the twenty-first century. Both quantum mechanics and dharmic philosophy believe the following:

1. The fragmentary and objective nature of the phenomenal world is illusory.
2. There is no absolute reality that is consistent for all.
3. There is no absolute time or space.
4. Time is not continuous; it is a series of moments.
5. Each person's reality is unique and is based on that person's perceptions and experiences.
6. The world is one unified and interrelated existence.

PAUSE TO REFLECT

Pause and reflect on what you have read in this chapter. Are you interested in finding out more about Hinduism, Buddhism, Vedānta, or American transcendentalism? Do you understand the relationship between Vedic/dharmic philosophy and American transcendentalism or quantum mechanics? What do you think about the proposition that Vedānta is both part of Hinduism as well as its own stand-alone philosophy? Do you understand how the concepts of dharma, māyā, and non-dualism are distinctly different from Western values? Think about your reaction to these new terms. Are you intrigued, or do you find the concepts off-putting? If off-putting, consider the reasons why you find them objectionable.

CHAPTER 11

Two Views of Reality

How do you see the world? Do you believe that the only reality is the world around you, the one you see, hear, smell, touch, and taste? To most people in the West, the objective reality they perceive through their senses is understood and assumed to be the true reality. It is the reality that Galileo and Newton measured and defined. It is the reality you experience every day. It is the one that you, as a unique individual, confront; the one in which you must interact with other unique individuals. You are pitted against the world "out there," including all the other people in it. It is also a world that has shaped and contained all that you have known and experienced. It is all you know. Scientists and philosophers refer to this world as "objective reality" or "Newtonian reality." It is what Eastern philosophers call a dualist view of the world; each individual is separate from and in conflict with the rest of the world.

That view is not the only view of reality. To most people in the East, the objective view of reality that our senses perceive does exist, but it is not the true reality. Most Easterners believe true reality is beyond the limitations of an individual's perceptions. It is one in which the differences between individuals melt away, and the differences between people, other sentient beings, and non-sentient objects also melts away. It is an undifferentiated whole in which each individual is an equal but superficially unique part of the whole. To the Eastern philosophers, this view is known as a non-dualist view. True reality is singular and comprehensive; humans are unique manifestations within the whole. There is no "I" that is separate from the rest of existence. It is non-dualist.

This abstract discussion is interesting, but what does it have to do with leadership? *Everything!* The leader's core values, the leader's perception of self, how the leader interacts with people, and how the leader uses natural resources are all shaped by the leader's view of reality. This chapter explores two differing views of reality in more detail.

THE WESTERN, OBJECTIVE VIEW OF REALITY

The dominant view of reality in the West developed in the period between the Renaissance and the Age of Enlightenment, roughly between the mid 1400s CE and the start of the French Revolution in 1789 CE. A series of discoveries and related philosophical thought built upon each other to create a view of reality that is objective and measurable. As Western Europe emerged from the Middle Ages, philosophy changed from a focus on the relationship of humanity with the divine to a focus on the importance and uniqueness of the individual human being. The terms "humanism" and "humane letters," connoting the emphasis on human writing on topics other than the scriptures, became the norm. In the visual arts, painters such as Peter Paul Rubens, Caravaggio, Jan Vermeer, and Rembrandt began to paint portraits of average people in everyday settings, rather than painting religious-oriented scenes. The portraits of these common people were painted in a more lifelike style than the former religious paintings and conveyed a sense of depth and three-dimensional perspective. Around 1435 CE, artists developed scientific perspective, a method to lay out a painting geometrically to create the correct illusion of three-dimensional perspective.

Developments in science provided the greatest impact on the perception of reality. The research of Galileo Galilei and Sir Isaac Newton, in particular, had significant influence on other scientists and philosophers. Galileo identified physical laws that pertained to falling objects and to the motion of a pendulum. With his development of the telescope, he was able to confirm the Copernican theory that the Earth and the other planets revolved around the sun, a position that put him on the wrong side of the Inquisition. Newton became symbolic of the era as a result of his research, which created a paradigm shift in how the world was perceived. From the work of Galileo, Newton, and the mathematician René Descartes came the image of the world as a Great Machine or "clockwork." Western thought and perception of reality became dominated by an emphasis on science, rational thought, and observation, rather than on experience and realization.

CHARACTERISTICS OF THE WESTERN, NEWTONIAN VIEW OF REALITY

Objective Reality and Rational Order

The dominant characteristic of the Western view of reality is the perception that the objective reality that can be perceived through the senses (including the use of telescopes and electron microscopes) is the only reality. Additionally, that objective reality is constructed in a comprehensible and rational order.

The most frequently used analogy is that of an internal clock mechanism.

The universe is seen as a set of building blocks. Electrons move around the nucleus of the atom. Atoms combine to make unique molecules, and molecules into cells. Cells combine to make uniquely identifiable objects and beings that form the Earth. The Earth and other planets circle the sun. The Solar System revolves within the Milky Way. The Milky Way is one of countless defined galaxies within the universe. From this perspective, every individual sentient being and non-sentient object was viewed as a uniquely individual entity built up from common building blocks. Each individual had its own unique shape with identifiable features.

As the scientific method became the dominant view of reality, greater emphasis was placed not only on observation, but also on the repeatability of the observation by another researcher. To be considered valid, a particular observation must be measurable and repeatable by another party. This emphasis on empirical and rational methods has resulted in a general perception that experimental results must satisfy common sense; that is, they must meet a preconceived notion of reality as a giant machine running like clockwork.

Continuous Experience

The research of Galileo, Newton, and other early scientists developed the theory that both time and motion are constant, continuous, and consistent for everyone. For that reason, continuity of experience became an important element in the view of individuals as independent entities with unique experiences within a uniformly consistent milieu of time and motion. Changes in entities, such as the progression from birth to death, were observed, but they were viewed as a continuum of time. Not only did each individual entity have its own unique set of physical features, but it also had its own unique set of thoughts and experiences.

Dualism

In the Western view, each sentient being and each non-sentient object is an independent entity with its own existence. This perception creates a duality in the perception of the physical environment. Rather than seeing themselves as an integral part of an interconnected whole, individuals see themselves as independent beings who are potentially in conflict with nature and other people. This sense of separation, combined with a focus on self-interest, has created many circumstances in which individuals and societies of like-minded individuals exploit natural resources and other people for personal gain.

The dualist point of view not only separates the individual from the rest of existence, it also separates the individual's physical existence from the metaphysical. The objective view of the world shapes how people react to the world. Only what is perceived to be observable and measurable is viewed as the "real world." The thoughts and values generated in the individual's mind, especially spiritual values, are treated as elements that cannot be empirically tested; therefore, they are treated as foreign and separate from the true, objective, and rational reality.

Dominance over the Physical Environment

The perception that the "I" is separate from the rest of existence can have a very negative impact. For the most part, scientific objectivity has had a beneficial impact on humanity. Without scientific discoveries, the world would not have had the technological breakthroughs that have significantly improved the quality of life that humans experience today. The emphasis on a fragmentary view of existence, however, has had a significant impact on the way humans treat the natural world and each other. The rise of pollution, the use of strip mining to extract cheap energy, and the clear cutting of virgin forests for lumber are but three examples of an indifferent view of the physical environment. Humanity's domination of the natural world for its own benefit at the expense of other sentient beings can be attributed to the fragmentary view of existence.

The separation of the "I" from the rest of the world "out there" also creates conflict among humans and creates a mindset that other humans can be exploited. This view has been a source of the tension among social groups worldwide, based on differences in race, religion, and social structure. This fragmentary and isolated view also creates problems at the individual level. A focus on the individual self and a desire to benefit the individual can lead to exploitation of other, less fortunate individuals. Throughout the world today, sweatshops and agricultural businesses employ children to produce clothing and other items or to harvest crops for the citizens of developed countries. Such a fragmentary view has created ethnic cleansing, a too frequently used method for eradicating groups of people who are "different" from the aggressors and has allowed unscrupulous corporate leaders to morally and financially bankrupt corporations to increase their personal wealth.

THE DHARMIC VIEW OF REALITY

The Western, Newtonian view of reality presents a perspective that sees the perceived world as the only reality. It is objective, measurable, and rational. Observers have the capacity to observe the actions without altering the outcomes. All sentient beings and non-sentient objects in this reality are independent entities that move continuously through time. Time is consistent and uniform for all entities.

The dharmic view of reality presents a very different view of reality. In the dharmic view, the ultimate reality includes all sentient beings and non-sentient objects as equal manifestations of a single, all-pervasive holistic reality. This ultimate reality is beyond the perception of humans. The world, as perceived by humanity, is recognized as part of the ultimate reality, but fragmentary constructs and perceptions of separate entities are recognized as limitations of the senses. This sensory-limited reality (the same as the objective reality in the Western view) is seen as illusion, in the dharmic view.

In contrast to the Western view, the dharmic view of reality places an emphasis on the unity and interconnectedness of all beings, rather than emphasizing the uniqueness of the individual. Since the observer is embedded in the reality and is a part of it, the observer cannot be an unbiased observer; reality can be realized only through experience, not unbiased observation. Additionally, in contrast to the Western view, time and experience are not continuous and constant; every moment is a new experience.

Characteristics of the Dharmic View of Reality

Non-dualism and Ultimate Reality

For a Westerner, a good starting point for understanding the concept of non-dualism is the quote by John Muir, "When we try to pick out anything by itself, we find it hitched to everything else in the universe."[33] This is a simplistic, but succinct, definition of non-dualism. In the dharmic view, there is no separation between one individual and the rest of humanity; neither is there a separation between humanity and the rest of the physical environment or between the physical and metaphysical. In stanzas 29–31 of the sixth lesson of the Bhagavad-Gita, Krishna presents the concept of unity to Arjuna by stating that the devoted man understands the unity of life. He sees all creatures as equal and part of a unified whole.

These three stanzas also refer to another important aspect of the perception of unity and non-dualism, which is the unity between all of existence in the perceived world and an underlying, common ultimate reality. In dharmic philosophy, the absolute, ultimate reality is Brahman. Unlike Christianity, in which God is presented in an anthropomorphic image, Brahman is presented as the generating force underlying all of creation. Within Christianity, there is a separation between God, the world, and man. God created the world and then man. All three are distinct, and each individual is a distinct soul. In the dharmic philosophy, the entire universe is a manifestation of Brahman. Within Vedānta, the phenomenal world and all sentient beings are projections of the ultimate reality that the beings can perceive. Just as humans cannot see the entire visible spectrum and cannot hear the entire sound spectrum, they cannot perceive all the layers or manifestations of Brahman.

Within the dharmic philosophy, each individual has a soul or "self" that is known as the Ātman. The Ātman and Brahman are regarded as one—or more accurately, as "not two." The relationship between the Ātman and Brahman has been described by Vivekananda with following analogy:

> As when the sun shines upon millions of globules of water, upon each particle is seen a most perfect representation of the sun, so the one Soul, the one Self, the one Existence of the universe, being reflected on all these numerous globules of varying names and forms, appears to be various. But it is in reality only one.[34]

The Dalai Lama gave another poetic view of the relationship between Brahman and Ātman with the description of "an infinite net of gems called 'Indra's jeweled net,' which reaches out to infinite space."[35] The Dalai Lama describes the net in more detail:

> At each knot on the net is a crystal gem, which is connected to all the other gems and reflects in itself all the others. On such a net, no jewel is in the center or at the edge. Each and every jewel is at the center, in that it reflects all the other jewels on the net. At the same time, it is at the edge, in that it is itself reflected in all the other jewels.[36]

Māyā—the Illusion of the Phenomenal World

The Newtonian view of reality perceives the phenomenal world (the world perceived through the senses) as the only reality, one that is objective and rational. Dharmic philosophy does not deny the existence of the phenomenal world, but it does not regard it as the only reality or even the ultimate reality. Māyā means illusion. Within dharmic philosophy, the phenomenal world is viewed as illusion on multiple levels.

As noted earlier, dharmic philosophy believes all of existence is interconnected and is a manifestation of Brahman, the ultimate reality. The most obvious level of illusion is the perception that the phenomenal world, dominated by fragmented objects, is the primary reality. Dharmic philosophers realized that humans were limited by their senses. There are limitations on what people can see, hear, taste, smell, and feel. As a result of those limitations, it is understandable that humans divide and separate the universe into objects; this separation allows them to reduce the complexity to manageable proportions.

Taking the concept of an illusory, fragmented reality a step further, some philosophers note that there is a more abstract view of illusion. This scenario is derived from the fact that all of an individual's perception of the world is through the senses. The red rose that a person sees is the result of light waves registering on the retina with the response registering in the brain. The person recognizes the image in the mind as a red rose because experience has taught the brain to remember the image of a red rose. The image of a particular red rose, however, is not the same for each person. One person may be color blind; the red registers differently in the person's brain. Another person may have a positive image of the rose, because memories of red roses are linked to a loved one. The next person, however, may have a negative image of a red rose, because he remembers getting stuck by a thorn. In each case, there is a different perception of existent reality. Reality becomes a creation of each individual mind. If each person has his or her own view of reality, there can be no objective reality. The perception of a common reality "out there" is an illusion.

A third level of illusion is the illusion of the independent "I," the independent ego or consciousness. Humans tend to perceive themselves as an individual being with an individual consciousness (self) that is enclosed in a unique body that reacts to a world "out there." "Effectively, the notion of intrinsic, independent existence is incompatible with causation. This is because causation implies contingency and dependence, while anything that possesses independent existence would be immutable and self-enclosed."[37] The Dalai Lama continues, "Anything that exists and has an identity does so only within the total network of everything that has a possible or potential relation to it. No phenomenon exists with an independent or intrinsic identity."[38] The illusion of the independent self with feelings, needs, and desires, according to the dharmic view, is the most insidious form of illusion. According to dharmic philosophy, the emphasis on the individual consciousness and its perceived needs leads to the suffering and pain found in life. This aspect of suffering is addressed in more detail later in this chapter.

Each Moment Is a Unique Experience

The Newtonian view of reality assumes that experiences are continuous and flow uniformly and cohesively through time. The dharmic view is very different. Dharmic philosophy believes that experience is not continuous and it is not directly connected to time. In the dharmic view, each current experience is colored by each individual's sensory perceptions and the individual's prior experiences and values; therefore, every moment is a new experience. No moment is identical in time or composition. "Attention shows that a given moment cannot be fixed exactly in relation to *time* (e.g., by the clock) but rather, that it covers some vaguely defined and somewhat variable extended period of duration."[39] The perception that each moment is a unique experience is one of the most important dharmic values for a leader. Leaders must make decisions; the manner in which reality is perceived alters how a leader will make decisions.

A contemporary example of the momentary and variable nature of experience in a business environment occurs in professional football. At the beginning of a season, a team creates a playbook; a selection of set plays that will be used in specific situations. The playbook is analogous to procedures manuals in other businesses. The playbook (procedures) establishes a common methodology for all constituents for achieving long-term goals (the championship), mid-range goals (the game), and short-term goals (progressing the ball forward on each down). During a game, each play is a unique moment. The quarterback (leader of the offense) selects a play (procedure) that is appropriate for that down, yardage needed, and location on the field. Even though the play is "standard," that particular moment is unique. The quarterback must account for the skills and health of his players on the field, the individual skills and health of the competitors, the defensive alignment selected by the competitors, environmental factors (weather and condition of the field), and the momentum of the game. The quarterback may decide to change the play; to call an audible seconds before the ball is snapped by the center. The ability of the leader to analyze the variable conditions at that moment, to make adjustments, and to direct the team's actions in implementing the play impacts the success of achieving the short-term goal. The success of the leader (quarterback) depended upon the leader's ability to understand the variables of that particular moment and adjust procedures to achieve success.

The difficulty with human life is that people are not born with an owner's manual or a road map. As a result, life is a series of decisions—both big and small. Every moment is a decision point. Some decision points are minor—"What will I eat for dinner?"—while others are major—"Where will I live? How will I earn money?" Humans must analyze their circumstances and make decisions. This is the crux of the story of the Bhagavad-Gita. It is not about the decision to go to war; it is Arjuna's basic decision of what to do next and how to muster the strength to make the decision. Arjuna is mired in despair as a result of his inability to assess the situation and respond with a proper plan of action.

Understanding through Experience and Realization

The Newtonian view of reality emphasizes understanding reality through observation and measurement. The dharmic view of reality emphasizes understanding through experience and realization. Understanding of reality cannot be intellectualized; it must be internally realized. The experiences may come about by interacting with the outside world or exploration of an individual's inner self through meditation. The experience breeds realization—realization of the unity of all sentient and non-sentient beings or the realization of the unity in the individual self (Ātman) with the ultimate reality (Brahman). These experiences are fleeting but have a powerful impact on the individual. The fleeting nature of these moments of experience was characterized in the "Ramayana" by the images of Rāmā, Sita, and Laksman walking on a narrow and winding jungle path. Rāmā takes the lead, and Laksman is at the rear. As a result of his devotion to his brother, Laksman wants to stay in visual contact with Rāmā. This vignette also has a symbolic meaning. Rāmā represents Brahman; Sita represents māyā; and Laksman represents Ātman. As they walk along the path, Laksman can sometimes see Rāmā. At other times, Sita (the illusion of māyā) blocks Laksman's view of Rāmā. Laksman, the individual manifestation, desires to see Rāmā, the undifferentiated whole. Sita—māyā resulting from human perceptual and cognitive limitations—prevents the individual manifestation from seeing the undifferentiated whole at will.

Jiddu Krishnamurti made the distinction between observation and experience when he wrote that the gathering of facts is not the same as understanding. "Knowledge does not lead to understanding; but understanding may enrich knowledge, and knowledge may implement understanding."[40]

Unique Perspectives and Diversity

The Newtonian view of reality believes that reality is objective and consistent with all observers. The dharmic view does not believe in an objective reality as the true reality. Since reality is experiential, every person creates his or her own reality. If all people create their own reality, there is no common, objective reality. The dharmic view of reality is an applicable alternative view in today's world in response to the concerns of Marshall McLuhan and Quentin Fiore. "Survival is not possible if one approaches his environment, the social drama, with a fixed, unchangeable point of view—the witless repetitive response to the unperceived."[41]

According to Krishnamurti, "The world is of our own making; the world is us, and we are the world."[42] Each person's world is made from his or her own experiences, attitudes, capabilities, occupation, and physical surroundings. This combination shapes and defines each person's reality. As a result, each person's reality is unique; there is no common reality.

This acceptance of a reality that is experience based and molded by each individual into a unique perspective also accepts diversity as an integral part of the dharmic philosophy of reality. If all the gems on Indra's net of gems are equal, but each of those gems varies in experience and attitude, the philosophy allows for a diversity of perspectives within a common unity. Vivekananda characterized this diversity as seeing the light from the sun through stained glass. The uniform light projected through each pane is shaded by the color (the attitudes, skills, and experiences) of that pane. The equality of individuals as a result of the underlying unity of existence gives credence to the value of diverse perceptions of reality.

The Randomness and Uncertainty of Constant Change

Many people see change as not part of the norm, not part of the daily operations of an organization. Leaders and managers try to control change, curtail it, create committees to study it, and otherwise treat it as an unforeseen external force thwarting the smooth and consistent flow of the well-oiled organization.

The dharmic view of change is very different. A key element of the dharmic view of reality is the impermanence of all existence. Constant change is considered the norm. Nothing is static; nothing is abiding. At every level of the existent world, change is constant. Continents are moving and mountains are eroding. Creatures are born, change through life, grow old, and die. Change is perceived most easily at the gross level. People notice that their bodies change over time; in adulthood they do not have the same body they had when they were children. Everything people experience is constantly changing. Their physical environment, emotions, sensory receptions, desires, and needs are in constant flux from moment to moment.

It is important for the leader to recognize that change is integral to existence and integral to the operation of an organization. Employees change. Markets change. Regulations change. Competitors change. The actual change that will occur cannot be foreseen. While the leader may not know when the market will change or when a key employee will resign, the leader can establish an organization that is mentally prepared to react flexibly to changes as they occur.

Good and Evil Together

In the Newtonian view of reality, good and evil are viewed as an either/or situation. A person or a situation is viewed as essentially good or evil. Within the dharmic view of reality, good and evil are viewed as equally necessary and relative to each other. The character of man is defined by his actions and his tendencies, both good and bad. Both good and evil have an equal share in defining that character. As man gains knowledge, he gains a greater understanding of where he is heading and where he has gone off the path. According to John Burroughs, both good and evil are necessary for character growth. "As the life of the globe depends upon degrees of heat and cold, depends upon differences, fluctuations, inequalities, so human development depends upon a mixture of good and evil."[43] With knowledge, man learns from his good and bad experiences. Each person has the potential for good as well as for bad.

The ethical challenges of the relative nature of good and evil are characterized well in the Bhagavad-Gita. The setting for the Bhagavad-Gita is an impending battle between warring cousins. It is also an appropriate setting to see that good and evil are relative. Arjuna is poised between two warring armies with friends and family on both sides. The fratricidal nature of the war accentuates the contradictions of conflict. Good and evil are not mutually exclusive; all good contains a little evil, and all evil contains a little good. Leaders may not face crises at the scale of a war, but they do face conflicts in which the trade-offs of positive impacts (good) and negative impacts (evil) must be assessed before deciding on the most appropriate action.

Wind farms using very large wind turbines have become a popular alternative to fossil fuels in the generation of electricity. Large installations with dozens of wind turbines are now located in the consistently windy Great Plains from North Dakota to Texas. The size of each wind turbine must be viewed in context. These units are nothing like the wind mills historically seen on family farms or seen in Dutch paintings. Large wind turbines capable of generating 2.0 to 3.5 megawatts of electricity stand approximately 300 feet high at the center of the rotor. The diameter of the rotors range from approximately 300 to 400 feet; the area covered by the rotation of the rotor is larger than a football field. Wind turbine technology has obvious benefits for society. As a non-polluting, renewable source of energy, wind power has inherent benefits in comparison to nuclear energy, coal, natural gas, and oil. Even with wind energy, however, there are negative impacts that must be considered. The large rotor blades pose an environmental threat to birds. For obvious reasons, wind farms are located in visually prominent areas, especially on hillsides. As a result, the wind turbines are visible for miles surrounding the farm. Many adjacent property owners object to the installations, citing visual pollution of relatively undisturbed rural locations. Wind farms are typically in remote, rural locations. The infrastructure required to transmit the electricity from the farm to the general grid is expensive and is seen as a negative factor contributing to additional visual pollution of the landscape extending from the installation. The negative factors do not necessarily diminish the validity of the positive factors. The dharmic leader must recognize that there will be both positive and negative factors in any situation requiring analysis and implementation. Efforts can be made to minimize the impact of the negatives, but the dharmic leader recognizes that negative elements will always exist.

In dharmic philosophical texts, the person who has come to personify the capacity of good and evil in each person is Queen Kaikeyi in the "Ramayana." Kaikeyi is one of three wives of King Dasaratha and the mother of Bharat. Even though she was not Ramā's natural mother, the mother/son relationship between Kaikeyi and Ramā was stronger than Ramā's bond with his own mother or Kaikeyi's bond to her natural son, Bharat. This love and devotion shown by Kaikeyi to Ramā represents Kaikeyi's capacity for good. Kaikeyi's capacity for evil was demonstrated by her demand that her son, Bharat, be made king and that Ramā be banished to the forest for fourteen years. This action caused an emotional rift in the family, the early death of King Dasaratha, and the enmity of the citizens of the kingdom.

The evil action by Kaikeyi in the "Ramayana" and the personal pain she later suffered from the consequences are reinforced in stanza 165 of the "Dhammapada," when it states that everyone chooses to be pure or impure, and no one can purify another person.

PAUSE TO REFLECT

This chapter presented a more in-depth comparison between the Newtonian and dharmic views of reality. After reading this chapter and referring to Table 1, does the difference in perspective make sense? What are your views? How do you view reality? Are you interested in the dharmic view and wish to research it further? Do you see how the two views of reality could produce differing perspectives on how to interact with other people or with the natural environment?

If you have read this book sequentially and did not jump around, you have now completed this book. Take time to reflect on the dharmic leadership model in its entirety. Does the model make sense to you? Does it present a cohesive and holistic methodology for leading other people with equality, equanimity, and humility? Has the material in this book caused you to reassess your values and behaviors? Most importantly, will the material in the book set you free or leave your free? Are you a dharmic leader?

Endnotes

[1] J. Krishnamurti, *Commentaries on Living: First Series* (Madras, India: Krishnamurti Foundation India, 1996). p. 82.

[2] S. Vivekananda, *The Complete Works of Swami Vivekananda*, Subsidized ed., 8 vols., vol. 1 (Calcutta: Advaita Ashrama, 1992; repr., Fifth). p. 32.

[3] Ibid. p. 27.

[4] Krishnamurti, *Commentaries on Living: First Series*. p. 113.

[5] Vivekananda, *The Complete Works of Swami Vivekananda*. pp. 56-57.

[6] *The Dhammapada.*, trans. Eknath Easwaran (Tomales, CA: Nilgiri Press, 1985).

[7] ———, *The Complete Works of Swami Vivekananda*. p. 29.

[8] Max De Pree, *Leadership Is an Art* (New York: Dell Publishing, 1989).

[9] ———, *Leadership Jazz* (New York: Dell Publishing, 1992).

[10] ———, "The Leader's Legacy," *Leader to Leader* 6(Fall 1997).

[11] Krishnamurti, *Commentaries on Living: First Series*.

[12] Tenzin Gyatso, *Many Ways to Nirvana: Reflections and Advice on Right Living* (New York: Penguin Compass, 2004). p. 116.

[13] Ibid.

[14] J. Krishnamurti, *Commentaries on Living: Second Series* (Madras, India: Krishnamurti Foundation India, 1995). p. 82.

[15] R. Buckminster Fuller, Jerome Agel, and Quentin Fiore, *I Seem to Be a Verb* (New York: Bantam Books, 1970). p. 1.

[16] Gyatso, *Many Ways to Nirvana: Reflections and Advice on Right Living*. p. 161.

[17] Krishnamurti, *Commentaries on Living: First Series*. p. 70.

[18] *Easwaran translation*. p. 148, #222.

[19] Ian McHarg, *Design with Nature* (New York: Wiley & Sons, 1992).

[20] Tenzin Gyatso, *Ethics for the New Millennium* (New York: Riverhead Books, 1999). p. 161.

[21] Vivekananda, *The Complete Works of Swami Vivekananda*.

[22] Ralph Waldo Emerson, *Journals of Ralph Waldo Emerson - 1820-1872 - vol. V* (McCutchen Press, 2007). p. 359.

[23] Tenzin Gyatso, *Freedom in Exile: The Autobiography of the Dalai Lama* (New York: HarperCollins Publishers, 1990). p. 269.

[24] John Burroughs, *The Writings of John Burroughs: Whitman: A Study.*, Riverby ed., vol. XVI, The writings of John Burroughs (New York: Houghton Mifflin, 1904). p. 32.

[25] John Muir, *My First Summer in the Sierra* (New York: Houghton Mifflin, 1998). p. 157.

[26] McHarg, *Design with Nature*. p. 5.

[27] Muir, *My First Summer in the Sierra*. p. 24.

[28] John Burroughs, *The Writings of John Burroughs: Under the Apple-Trees.*, Riverby ed., vol. XIX (New York: Houghton Mifflin, 1916). pp. 58-59.

[29] Henry David Thoreau, *The Portable Thoreau* (New York: Penguin Books, 1981). p.117.

[30] Burroughs, *The Writings of John Burroughs: Whitman: A Study*.

[31] Walt Whitman, *Leaves of Grass* (New York: The New American Library, 1958). p. 49, stanza 1.

[32] Ibid. p. 64, stanza 20.

[33] Muir, *My First Summer in the Sierra*. p. 157.

[34] Vivekananda, *The Complete Works of Swami Vivekananda*. p. 275.

[35] Tenzin Gyatso, *The Universe in a Single Atom: The Convergence of Science and Spirituality* (New York: Morgan Road Books, 2005). p. 89.

[36] Ibid.

[37] Ibid. p. 47.

[38] Ibid. p. 64.

[39] David Bohm, *Wholeness and the Implicate Order* (New York: Routledge Classics, 2005). p. 259.

[40] J. Krishnamurti, *Commentaries on Living: Third Series* (Madras, India: Krishnamurti Foundation India, 1995). p. 4.

[41] Marshall McLuhan and Quentin Fiore, *The Medium is the Massage* (New York, NY: Bantam Books, 1967). p. 10.

[42] Krishnamurti, *Commentaries on Living: Third Series*. p. 96.

[43] John Burroughs, *The Writings of John Burroughs: The Light of Day.*, Riverby ed., vol. XVII (New York: Houghton Mifflin, 1904). p. 174.

References

Bohm, David. *Wholeness and the Implicate Order.* New York: Routledge Classics, 2005.

Burroughs, John. *The Writings of John Burroughs: The Light of Day.* Riverby ed. Vol. XVII, New York: Houghton Mifflin, 1904.

———. *The Writings of John Burroughs: Under the Apple-Trees.* Riverby ed. Vol. XIX, New York: Houghton Mifflin, 1916.

———. *The Writings of John Burroughs: Whitman: A Study.* The Writings of John Burroughs. Riverby ed. Vol. XVI, New York: Houghton Mifflin, 1904.

De Pree, Max. "The Leader's Legacy." *Leader to Leader* 6 (Fall 1997): 18-23.

———. *Leadership Is an Art.* New York: Dell Publishing, 1989.

———. *Leadership Jazz.* New York: Dell Publishing, 1992.

The Dhammapada. Translated by Eknath Easwaran. Tomales, CA: Nilgiri Press, 1985.

Emerson, Ralph Waldo. *Journals of Ralph Waldo Emerson — 1820-1872 - Vol. V.* McCutchen Press, 2007.

Fuller, R. Buckminster, Jerome Agel, and Quentin Fiore. *I Seem to Be a Verb.* New York: Bantam Books, 1970.

Gyatso, Tenzin. *Ethics for the New Millennium.* New York: Riverhead Books, 1999.

———. *Freedom in Exile: The Autobiography of the Dalai Lama.* New York: HarperCollins Publishers, 1990.

———. *Many Ways to Nirvana: Reflections and Advice on Right Living.* New York: Penguin Compass, 2004.

———. *The Universe in a Single Atom: The Convergence of Science and Spirituality.* New York: Morgan Road Books, 2005.

Krishnamurti, J. *Commentaries on Living: First Series.* Madras, India: Krishnamurti Foundation India, 1996.

———. *Commentaries on Living: Second Series.* Madras, India: Krishnamurti Foundation India, 1995.

———. *Commentaries on Living: Third Series.* Madras, India: Krishnamurti Foundation India, 1995.

McHarg, Ian. *Design with Nature.* New York: Wiley & Sons, 1992.

McLuhan, Marshall, and Quentin Fiore. *The Medium Is the Massage.* New York, NY: Bantam Books, 1967.

Muir, John. *My First Summer in the Sierra.* New York: Houghton Mifflin, 1998. 1911.

Thoreau, Henry David. *The Portable Thoreau.* New York: Penguin Books, 1981.

Vivekananda, S. *The Complete Works of Swami Vivekananda.* Subsidized ed. 8 vols. Vol. 1, Calcutta: Advaita Ashrama, 1992. Fifth.

Whitman, Walt. *Leaves of Grass.* New York: The New American Library, 1958.

www.ingramcontent.com/pod-product-compliance
Lightning Source LLC
Chambersburg PA
CBHW052050070526
44584CB00017B/2117